15 And he said unto them, Go ye into all the world, and preach the gospel to every creature. 16 He that believeth and is baptized shall be saved; but he that believeth not shall be damned. 17 And these signs shall follow them that believe: In my name shall they cast out devils; they shall speak with new tongues; 18 They shall take up serpents; and if they drink any deadly thing, it shall not hurt them; they shall lay hands on the sick, and they shall recover. 19 So then after the Lord had spoken unto them, he was received up into heaven, and sat on the right hand of God. 20 And they went forth, and preached every where, the Lord working with them, and confirming the word with signs following. Amen. (MARK 16:15-20.)   13 Is any among you afflicted? let him pray. Is any merry? let him sing psalms. 14 Is any sick among you? let him call for the elders of the church; and let them pray over him, anointing him with oil in the name of the Lord. (JAMES 5:13-14).   32 And whosoever speaketh a word against the Son of man, it shall be forgiven him: but whosoever speaketh against the Holy Ghost, it shall not be forgiven him, neither in this world, neither in the world to come. (MATTHEW 12:32).

To Ella Van Gilder

and our mothers, Nellie Benziger and Evelyn Creekmore

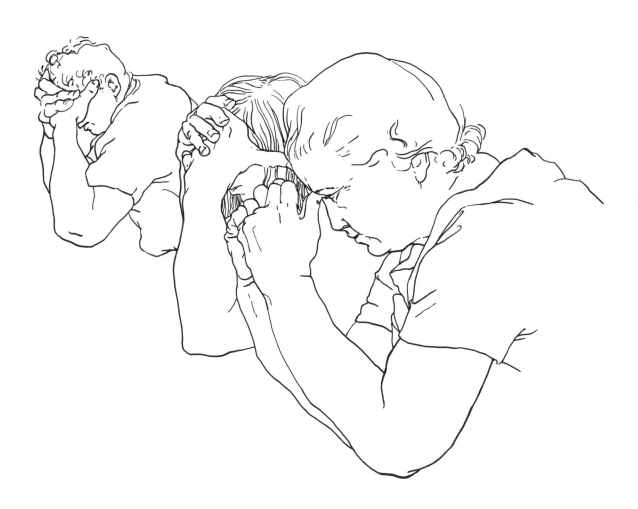

REVIVAL!

by

Eleanor Dickinson

text

Barbara Benziger

introduction by Walter Hopps

HARPER & ROW, PUBLISHERS

New York, Evanston, San Francisco, London

Wilt thou not revive us again: that thy people

In some cases, names have been changed in these quotations to protect the privacy of the worshipers.

Those wishing to study the original material upon which this book is based are referred to the following sources:

"Dickinson Collection of Revival Artifacts," the Smithsonian Institution, Washington, D.C.

"Revival Services in Tennessee, Kentucky, and West Virginia" tapes, Archive of Folk Songs, The Library of Congress, Washington, D.C.

"Dickinson Collection of Revival Hymnals," Music Division, The Library of Congress, Washington, D.C.

"Revival Drawings by Eleanor Dickinson" in the collections of The Library of Congress and the National Collection of Fine Arts, the Smithsonian Institution.

Drawings and photographs lent through the courtesy of The Poindexter Gallery, New York, and The William Sawyer Gallery, San Francisco.

Designed by Lydia Link

Library of Congress Cataloging in Publication Data

Dickinson, Eleanor, 1931-
  Revival.
  1. Revivals—Appalachian Mountains, Southern.
I. Benziger, Barbara. II. Title.
BV3774.A66D5   269'.2'097   73-18697
ISBN 0-06-061920-1
ISBN 0-06-061921-X (pbk.)

Acknowledgments

I would like to express my thanks to the many people who have had a part in the creation of REVIVAL! and especially to the following:

Walter Hopps, who, as director of The Corcoran Gallery of Art, first understood the idea and encouraged me in this unusual art form;

the preachers and people in East Tennessee, Kentucky, and West Virginia who welcomed me to their tents and churches and allowed me to draw, record, and photograph;

all the museum personnel who tackled a most unusual exhibit and installation;

the various directors of The Library of Congress and the Smithsonian Institution for their support and interest;

the publishers for their cooperation in developing this book as a total experience;

my family, friends and everyone who, during the last seven years, helped me collect the artifacts and other materials used here in the REVIVAL! exhibitions.

ELEANOR DICKINSON

in the midst of trouble, thou wilt revive me...

Introduction

Eleanor Dickinson has been deservedly acknowledged as one of the country's most powerful artists committed to figure drawing, and perhaps with no other subject matter in her career to date has her uniquely clear, strong, and austere approach to the medium found as appropriate a means of expression as in her *Revival!* drawings. There is in Dickinson's artistry and in the nature of the revival meetings themselves a union of simplicity of materials and setting combined with high emotional content and substance.

Elizabeth Coffelt has perceptively described Dickinson's work as intuitive and direct, involving great stillness and concentration. Undertaken with no preliminary sketches or even sketching motion common to the drawing experience, but rather with an "unbroken, fluid motion of her whole arm that describes a critical point of action," her technique involves the use of a felt-tip marking pen on large sheets of paper. She works as simply and quickly as possible with a sure, even, unbroken linear outline. It is the facial expression and bodily posture of her subjects that concern her; virtually no reference is made to her subjects' physical setting in the drawings. Coffelt, who has observed Dickinson at work, describes the process as follows: "The result is a gradual, almost imperceptible emergence of the image on paper; there seems to be little happening at first. It is much like watching the image emerge on sensitized paper in the darkroom. Magically, it is all there at once. And the drawing stops."

This book represents the current embodiment of an extraordinary project which began for Eleanor Creekmore Dickinson seven years ago in her native Knoxville, Tennessee. It was here that she visited a tent revival to draw the participants. The total engagement and highly charged passion of this revival meeting was of such impact to compel her, step by step, to absorb every aspect she possibly could of the phenomenon. As the project developed, she made hundreds of on-site figure drawings, hours of tape recordings of the services, photographed the settings as thoroughly as she might, and collected every sort of transportable object related to the revival manifestation: handbills, hymnals, signs, and all manner of ephemera.

Serious critics of Dickinson's work, while acknowledging the power and quality of her drawings, have taken exception to what seemed to them the superfluous environmental context in which the *Revival!* drawings are presented. Often they have been seemingly indifferent to the compelling documentary concerns developing with her artistry. On the occasion of this publication, it seems important to consider for a moment the spare tradition (and yet one of major consequence within American art) where esthetic and documentary functions have united.

One need only recall Audubon in the late 18th century—an artist's engagement with natural history; George Catlin in the early 19th century and his social documentation of the American Indians; Timothy O'Sullivan later in the 19th century as the great photo-journalist chronicler of our Civil War and later documentarian of the Far West. All of this work has long since assumed not only its place in the archives of social history but also on the walls of our art museums. Perhaps the greatest example in our time of the fully esthetic union of visual images, words, and data relating to specific members of our culture was created by James Agee and Walker Evans in their profoundly moving *Let Us Now Praise Famous Men*. It is in the context of such work that we might best view the achievement of Eleanor Dickinson's *Revival!*

There is a certain sadness within the tradition of work of which I have spoken. These phenomena—those of the animal kingdom, passionately regarded areas of our own culture, and of course the land itself—vanish even as we observe and reflect. Dickinson has commented:

> Although Pentecostal religion is steadily growing in the United States, every year there are fewer of the small revival tents. Many of the phenomena depicted may become extinct, as they are now remote. I was privileged to be the guest of these evangelical groups—to draw, photograph, and make tape recordings. I statisfied the evangelists and the people that my intent was artistic and documentary. Indeed, I believe they felt me to be a kind of missionary.

The first public manifestation of the *Revival!* project was organized by Nina Felshin for The Corcoran Gallery of Art in Washington, D.C. in September of 1970. This exhibition and its subsequent tour are described in the ensuing text, much of which was compiled from the over-200 hours of Dickinson's tapes of revival meetings. At the time, while on the staff of the Corcoran, I was enormously impressed, not only with the nature of Dickinson's total project, the exhibit itself, and her skill as an artist, but with her great patience and determination in bringing a unique project to fruition. While maintaining the distance necessary to function as artist and social documentarian (she has functioned throughout as a participant-observer much as an ethnologist engaged in field work), her own emotional involvement must be said to have often reached the peak and nature of that native to revivals. However, she has conscientiously sought to approach the subject with open, direct simplicity. It must be stressed that Dickinson's primary discipline is that of a graphic artist, and it is ultimately through an artist's eye that she has engaged in *Revival!*

WALTER HOPPS
NATIONAL COLLECTION OF FINE ARTS
SMITHSONIAN INSTITUTION

midst of the years... (HABAKKUK 3:2)   ...To

revive the spirit of the humble, and to revive

Contents

the heart of the contrite ones. (ISAIAH 57:15)

For where two or three are gathered together in

These are the people,
These are the faces,
These are the sounds of revivals
   held in tents in the Great Smoky Mountains.

Revival: An evangelical service specifically held
   to effect a religious awakening.

These are the people,
These are the faces
   which have been drawn and taped and assembled during several
   summers by Eleanor Dickinson, an artist who is deft with an intense,
   expressive, and brilliantly economical line.

They are strong, proud, hard-working, and quiet people,
   but they are transformed in their revivals,
   exalted, excited, emotional, buoyed by faith.

They believe God is using their bodies
   to act out some purpose.

When one of them has a revelation
   he is considered holy by the others.

They pray over someone believed to be possessed by devils,
   and cast out the devils.

They pray for the sick, expecting immediate healing
   if faith in God is strong enough.

They confess their sins and repent.
   They bear witness to what God has done in their lives.

Their feet are washed according to the
   Biblical description.

They prophesy in a trancelike state,
   speaking in the first person as if God himself were speaking.

And they sing,
   and they sing—songs and hymns.

They clap and they cry out.

Their towns are called Pigeon Forge, Goose Gap, Happy Hollow, Mucktown,
   Sunset Gap, Elkmont. Their churches are Baptist, Church of God,
   Assembly of God, Missionary Baptist, Primitive Baptist, and Holiness.
   They are white and black. . . .

       Introduction to the film, *Revival at the Corcoran*
       Aline Saarinen, ''The Today Show,'' NBC

my name, there am I in the midst of them.

Revive Us Again

When REVIVAL! by Eleanor Dickinson opened at the Corcoran Gallery of Art in Washington, D.C., the exhibit provided a sharp contrast to the formal museum setting. Eighty-four drawings, many larger than life, lined the walls, but each drawing was titled with the first few lines of a hymn which might be sung at a revival. In the center of the room wooden folding chairs were arranged as if in a revival tent. A Bible rested on a lectern facing the "congregation," and above it a twelve-foot red-and-white banner proclaimed: LORD SEND A REVIVAL. On the folding chairs were hymnals and paper fans. The hymnals were old, most of them long out of print. It was a warm night–appropriate since most revivals are held during the summer–and many visitors sat and fanned themselves. Some of the fans were old, some new. On one side of each was a religious picture, on the other usually a prayer along with an ad for a funeral parlor in a small southern town.

In an adjoining room were displayed various other artifacts such as posters and flyers announcing revivals, embroidered samplers, bumper stickers, and road signs, all bearing religious messages: PREPARE TO MEET GOD. JESUS IS COMING SOON. From a speaker system the authentic sounds of a revival meeting filled the gallery. The artist had also collected tape recordings of hymn singing, preaching, prayer, testifying, speaking "in other tongues," and–as is often the case in a revival tent–crying babies, barking dogs, and the sudden thunderstorms common to the Appalachian Mountains.

A previous opening had been held at the Dulin Gallery of Art in Knoxville, Tennessee. There, as in Washington, some came to look at art work and others to worship. Students from the state university called it a trip or a happening. Others wept. Sometimes a visiting preacher delivered a sermon. Later REVIVAL! toured the country, and it was viewed differently by many different groups of people. The artist always insisted on only one thing: that it was more than a show of drawings. Perhaps the truth is that by exhibiting the portraits of her people in the setting in which she found them, Eleanor Dickinson had recreated a revival.

For a number of summers she traveled in rural and urban areas of Tennessee, Kentucky, and West Virginia, drawing from life as the people worshiped in tents and churches, as they sang, prayed, danced, or in many cases sat quietly listening. She attended literally hundreds of revival meetings as well as footwashing ceremonies, prayer services, and baptisms in creeks and rivers. Sometimes she spent the whole day at a revival. There might be a prayer meeting in the afternoon, an evening song service, and perhaps "dinner on the grounds" served in between. The preachers she heard were both black and white, men and

out of great tribulation, and have washed their

No. 126. Lord Send a Revival.

J. M. H.   J. M. Henson

1. We meet in Thy tem-ple dear Lord to pray For pow-er di-vine in the
2. Our hearts have grown cold and we stand a-far Not knowing how far from the
3. We fall at Thy feet now oh, God of love, And plead for the pow'r from Thy

old-time way; Oh, send a re-vi-val of grace and love, That
goal we are; Oh, draw us much clos-er dear Lord to Thee, That
throne a-bove; Oh, help us to hum-ble our-selves this hour, And

REFRAIN.

com-eth to us from Thy throne a-bove.
ser-vants of Thine we may ev-er be. Oh, send a re-vi-val to-
send a re-vi-val of love and pow'r.   Oh,

day,.............. En-dow us with pow-er we pray;.............. That
send it to-day,   Thy pow-er we pray;

we may re-new our love and be true, Oh, send a re-vi-val to-day.

J. M. Henson, owner.

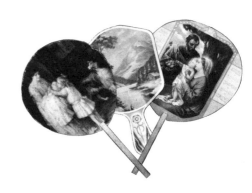

2

robes, and made them white in the blood of the

women. Some of the revivals she visited were independent. Others were sponsored by churches, including Baptist, Church of God, Missionary Baptist, Primitive Baptist, Assembly of God, Holiness, and others. Their religious customs differ greatly since, even within one denomination, the churches may emphasize different passages of scripture.

Often she was distrusted at first, but Dickinson had grown up in East Tennessee. She had attended a Baptist church as a child and later taught Sunday school for six years. She could sing the familiar hymns and discuss scripture with the preacher after a service. Although she had been away for a number of years, her speech soon regained something of the local accent, and it wasn't long before she was welcome to bring her drawing materials to revival meetings. Indeed, once she had satisfied the evangelists that her intent was artistic and documentary, many looked upon her as a kind of missionary.

She usually sat at one side of the congregation, working quickly with a felt-tipped pen on large sheets of paper clipped to a Masonite board. Sometimes she sat among the choir, and more than once under the piano. She dressed conservatively, partly in order to attract as little attention as possible, but also because many churches would have firmly disapproved of makeup, a short skirt or a woman in pants. After a while she realized that portraits of the people were not enough to create the total experience of a revival. It was then that she began carrying her tape recorder with her and also taking photographs whenever possible.

In her search for revival meetings, she made an effort to avoid the large tents of the popular traveling evangelists, but went instead to small Appalachian towns or the less prosperous neighborhoods of cities. In communities like Pigeon Forge, Valley Grove, Henderson Settlement, Bean Station, or Scrabble Creek, the financial rewards for a preacher are small. In fact, many of the preachers quoted here work at other full-time jobs. They may be laborers in mines or factories, or they may be in business. They may plow the land on their own farms. Some are employed all year round and hold revivals during their summer vacations. An offering is taken at every service, but most individuals can contribute little, and often the entire sum is needed for maintenance of the church or tent, utilities, and other such expenses. It is unlikely that these preachers are doing their work for commercial reasons.

For instance, there's **REV. PAPPY GUBE BEAVER** of the Holiness sect.

"No doubt John the Baptist, when he was in the wilderness crying out, he got discouraged, no doubt many times. He was in the wilderness crying out and telling people that they must be borned again and must be saved. See, they thought John was the Christ. But he told them he wasn't Him. He said, 'I'm the one crying in the wilderness. I'm the one that eats locusts and wild honey, preaching the word of God.' Thank God, I've got down to boloney and white bread a many a time. We've sat down along the road from some of the services where we've been, my wife and children, and we'd buy a loaf of bread and a big half a pound or pound of boloney. And I tell you we've enjoyed it. Well, we've had a good spiritual meeting somewhere, and we didn't have sufficient money to go to a big restaurant, and I thank God for that. We just sat down and enjoyed it. And the fact about it, sometimes I'd rather have some good boloney and a big head of onion to go with it than be in some of the restaurants—can you say Amen? Amen; it's better food, anyhow."

Rev. Beaver doesn't have a church, and he doesn't travel from town to town, but he is the proud owner of a new tent set up in a vacant lot on the side of a hill in the Lonsdale section of Knoxville, Tennessee. His tent is small, seating no more than a hundred people, but you can't miss its red-and-white stripes. The sides are blue and Rev. Pappy Beaver calls it his "tent of many colors." It's just off the freeway and you can park your car with the others on the hillside. As you enter the tent you'll notice that sawdust covers the ground. Toward the front you can see a wooden platform with a lectern. Nailed to the lectern are license plates with messages: JESUS SAVES and MEET ME IN CHURCH ON SUNDAY. Behind the lectern is a reproduction on velvet of the Last Supper. Some revivals last a week, some ten days or several weeks, but Reverend Beaver's revival goes on all summer with meetings three or four times a week. For many years, in order to support his religious activities, he worked every day driving a limousine between downtown Knoxville and the local airport.

"I got the name Pappy when my first child was born. I was on radio and they kept calling me Pappy. People say, 'Brother Pappy, you got enough labor trying to pay the rent, trying to buy these tents and things. Don't see how you do it. I'm sorry for you.'

"Well, I say, 'Just pray for me.' My mind and heart is upon the work of the Lord. Half the time when I'm driving my limousine to the airport, sometimes I'll be praying and having my mind in meditation on this revival. And I don't even know where I let my passengers out at. I'm a-praying that God would step out and give me this work to do altogether, so that I can get a little more rest in my body."

Since this sermon was preached, Reverend Beaver has been able to leave his driving job and devote full time to preaching—in his tent and on a daily radio program. His four children are grown and self-supporting now. Even so his wife, MILDRED BEAVER, admitted that at first she was afraid there wouldn't be enough money coming in to live on. Now, however, she smiles and states firmly, "We don't get too

hath not works, is dead, being alone. Yea, a man

Rock of Ages, cleft for me,
 Let me hide myself in Thee;
Let the water and the blood,
 From thy riven side which flowed,
Be of sin the double cure,
 Save me from its guilt and power.

much each month, me and my husband, but law, the Lord just makes a way for us.''

Reverend Beaver's tent isn't completely paid for yet, but so far he has met all the payments with contributions from the collection plate. And there is a new sign out front which Eleanor Dickinson painted and presented to him in exchange for his old one. She wanted the old sign to be among the artifacts she displayed with her drawings. Reverend Beaver and his congregation are happy with their new sign, but they have never quite understood the artist's strange practice of offering new signs for old.

Every Friday night Rev. Pappy Beaver holds what's called a "pounding." This is a custom handed down since the time when the frontier preachers first crossed the mountains, and it simply means that everyone who comes to the service that night brings a pound of sugar, coffee, vegetables, or other produce. In pioneer days many preachers supported their families in this way. Now Reverend Beaver frankly tells his congregation about his favorite brand of coffee and announces from the pulpit that he prefers dry cereal for breakfast.

ELZIE PREAST (*pronounced as in "priest"*) *is the overseer of a small church in Scrabble Creek, West Virginia. He, too, works for a living.*

"Brother, I'd rather dig a ditch. I'd rather drive a truck—and I've drove it for thirty-five years. I'd rather do that and preach what I feel and what I believe—glory to God—and what I've experienced, than to be paid to try to fool a lot of people and try to please a lot of people. I'm sorry for preachers that does it for an occupation. You know, when they move around, if they don't please the one that's got the longest tongue and the one that's got the longest nose—usually they don't stay very long. Because usually the one that's got about the longest tongue and the longest nose or got the pull or got the money, that's who they have to please. And I know how they work. This lady told me—this preacher's wife—she said, 'There's some of the nosiest people around here.' And they didn't stay there but a few months. She said, 'The only way I know of that this woman' (she spoke her name—it was a neighbor on the hill) 'the only way I know of that she could have known what kind of a princess-slip I had on is that she watched me through the bathroom window off the hill.' The house set down below, you know, and the other house is back up here. Said, 'That's the only way that I know that she could watch and know what kind of a princess-slip I had on, is for her to watch through the window and see it.' That's getting pretty rough, isn't it, for preachers' wives? That other woman thought she was wearing too loud a slip. A red slip. But it wouldn't make any difference to me tonight—if you've got a black one on I love black. And if you've got a white one on, I love white. So it doesn't make any difference to me whether it's red, white, blue, or black."

thy faith without thy works, and I will shew

When I can read my title clear,
To mansions in the skies,
I'll bid farewell to ev'ry fear,
And wipe my weeping eyes.

We'll stand the storm, We will anchor by and by.

thee my faith by my works. (JAMES 2:17-18)   Be ye

We're marching to Zion,
    Beautiful, beautiful Zion;
We're marching upward to Zion,
    The beautiful city of God.

therefore ready also: for the Son of man cometh

Elzie Preast's church is a small white frame building. There is no steeple or belfry, and the furnishings inside are bare essentials. It's approximately a sixty-mile drive over winding roads to Joe Turner's church on a steep hill at Camp Creek. Here a sign over the door reads simply JESUS CHURCH. In both these churches the believers handle poisonous snakes and drink strychnine to demonstrate their faith. They also dance; they greet one another with "a holy kiss" [I Corinthians 16:20]. Their revival services are without form, since they feel that worshipers should have absolute freedom to do as they like. In the following excerpt from a sermon at Camp Creek, JOE TURNER reveals much about his daily life as well as his religious beliefs.

"I've prayed—they've timed me before now—two solid hours and never stopped. I didn't know they was timing me. I didn't have no idea. I got on my knees, boy, and I prayed. Bless God. While the horses had stopped to rest, I'd pray. Amen. I'd tell my wife, 'I'm going a-hunting.' I wasn't interested in hunting. I'd go off up the hollow, and somebody said, 'Brother Turner, I heard you praying and praying and praying.' Praise God. I'd get me a drink of water at the spring, and I'd pray before drinking. After I'd drunk the water, I'd pray again. Thank God. Didn't take me long to pray. Amen. I'd thank God again. Brother, listen, I'd go out and pick up my coal out in the shed and I'd pray again. I'd get it in the house and I'd pray again. Oh, praise God tonight! The Bible says to praise him. I'll praise him and pray without ceasing. Glory hallelujah! Brother, if you'll do that tonight, you can get somewhere with God. Thank God!

"Why, up the hollow there—I live right at the forks of the hollow —and up the righthand fork you can go up there in a little old path. And there's a little old knoll there. It was about thirty or forty foot long and about forty or fifty foot wide, and it was just like going up on the cemetery. Glory to God, I prayed till God sanctified that piece of ground some way or other. Why, even the weeds quit growing on it for a while. Glory to God! That don't sound to be so—Amen. The weeds quit growing on it. Glory to God. It looked like a lawn of some kind that somebody had mowed down. Yeah, brother, that was the place —Amen—that I could get ahold of God.

"Listen, my friends, there's a man built a house right in above us. And he went for years before he completed it and moved in, and I didn't know why. And my wife would wake up sometimes of a night. And she'd come in the room and wake up the children. 'Go see where your daddy is.' Yeah, thank God, brother. I'd get up there in that old house—glory to God—a whole house! Glory to God! In the morning, Brother Delbert, I'd get on my knees, thank God, and say, 'Lord, I don't want to be deceived. I want something, and I—' And after a while the children would say, 'Mommie, he's up there praying.' "

at an hour when ye think not. (LUKE 12:40)

The lives of the people who attend revival meetings vary as do their occupations, the areas in which they live, and the individual beliefs of their churches. In the cities they may own their own homes or live in public housing. In rural areas they may live in cabins, farmhouses, or mobile homes. Both young and old come to church in great numbers. Many carry their own Bibles with them—perhaps dog-eared and worn. Some congregations, particularly far back in the Smoky Mountains, are exclusively white—usually because the black population in such areas is almost nonexistent. In urban areas, if a neighborhood is mostly black, there are black churches. However, most revivals are integrated.

When asked about his feelings on racial integration, **ELZIE PREAST** *replied,* "I preach that Jesus died to save all people that come unto him, regardless of skin. God bless your hearts. Yes, we've had colored people here. We believe in kissing and greeting one another with a holy kiss, and it wouldn't make any difference to me, black or white, if it's people filled with the Spirit of God. Bless the Lord. If Jesus baptizes you with the Holy Ghost tonight, who am I to say that I'm better than you are? That's the same Spirit. And it says the whole family, in heaven and in earth, is called by his name."

REV. HARLAN S. KARNES *is a visiting evangelist who preached at a tent revival sponsored by a Baptist church near Maryville, Tennessee.*

"Tonight we've got all kinds of people here. We've got some black people here. We got one of them in the choir. We've got some white people here. We've got some wealthy people here and we've got the people that can't even pay the rent that's here. People that's being evicted from their homes because they can't pay the rent. Now how're you going to minister to a group of people like that? Only one way. Jesus said, 'I come to minister to those people who need me.' And beloved, that's why I'm here. I've come for one thing. To preach and talk with people who need Jesus. And the man who don't need Jesus can see that. A saved man can see by wisdom the preaching of the gospel."

As people begin to fill up the chairs at a revival, the service may begin with music. The evangelist may sing alone or lead the congregation in several hymns. The sermon comes later and may be prepared but is often completely spontaneous. It will probably contain a good many Biblical quotations—not always accurate because in his excitement, the preacher usually does not stop to read but quotes from memory a passage of scripture to illustrate a point. Most sermons begin with a message of welcome to the congregation and visitors.

ELZIE PREAST: "I hope you feel welcome. This is not my church. I don't even claim it, only as a home church. It's not my congregation. I feel

Then there were brought unto him little children,

In that great gettin up morning
by and by, by and by,
Judgement coming, judgement coming,
I'll meet my Jesus in the sky.

that he should put his hands on them, and pray:

Stand up! Stand up for Jesus!
Ye soldiers of the Cross;
Lift high His royal banner,
It must not suffer loss;

and the disciples rebuked them. But Jesus said,

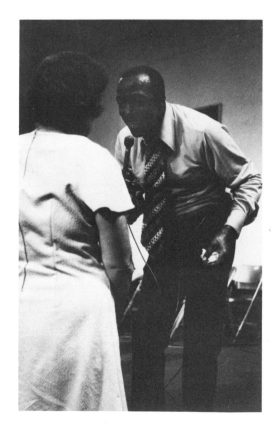

like you belong to the Lord. And I'm a part of you. I'm just a part of you. But this is not my church. I'm not the head of it. They crucified the leader of this church—bless the Lord—and we're depending on his Spirit tonight. Bless the Lord! May the Lord bless all of you. Do we have any people that's never been here before? Would you hold your hands up? We're glad you're here. I hope you feel welcome. I hope you hear something different than you've ever heard in your life. I hope you'll be like Mary was when they told her some things. Said she pondered it, didn't she? Pondered it in her heart. So you may hear something here tonight. Maybe you'll ponder it in your hearts and maybe you'll study it over. And after a while it may mean a lot to your soul in the end. Bless the Lord!''

JOE TURNER: "Oh, glory to God! I used to be a timber cutter. Amen. I used to be a saw-logger. And we'd go into the mountains, and we'd peck on a tree. It would look pretty good, but it would sound hollow. And we'd pass him on up. We'd let him stand. And that's what's wrong with a lot of church people tonight. They've lost their insides. Glory to God! I've said a lot of times, when you make a pie, you first fix up your dough. And you put it in a pan. And you'll put it into the stove and brown it. Then you'll bring it out and put your filling in it and stick it back in there. It becomes a pie!

"Out on the mountainside we can find trees that's green. When the wind blows, the oak trees will rock. And there's some there that's standing that's lost their power. They've lost their sap. When the wind blows they still stand there, a-pining awhile because they've lost the thing that makes them live. Amen. They've lost the sap that makes them live. When the sap goes dead in that tree, that tree dies. Amen. Its twigs, its leaves, will all fall off directly. The limbs begin to drop off small. And they're getting larger, and larger. Why? Because the tree's getting more rottener and rottener and rottener. Listen tonight, if you can feel any God in you at all, you ought to stir it up—glory to God! Amen. And listen tonight. And get joy tonight!''

AN INDEPENDENT EVANGELIST *preaching in a small tent near Middlesboro, Kentucky:* "I can tell we have some folks here tonight that love God. I can tell. I can tell you folks love Jesus. And you know, it's a miracle when a revival goes ten days or two weeks anymore. And when this keeps on going two and three and four weeks and people still love God enough to come out and worship Jesus, especially on a damp night under an old tent, they have to love God. Maybe that's the reason God honors these tent revivals so much—it's because you have to leave all your pride at home when you come out to a tent meeting, because you might step in a puddle of water, or there might be a few drops of water on the chair where you set down, or you might even—you ladies might snag your hose on a sticker weed or something. And so you can't have a whole lot of pride and come out to a revival service. And so, in spite of

Suffer little children, and forbid them not, to

all the adverse conditions, we'll just show God we love him enough that we want to come out and worship him. And I believe God honors it, don't you? Hallelujah! Hallelujah!''

Worshipers who come to revival meetings seeking help with earthly problems will find a strong sense of group support, but it is true that they must leave their pride at home, for they can expect no sense of privacy. Their drinking habits, their sex lives and other "backsliding conditions" are confessed and aired before the congregation. And the preacher's family is no exception. During one revival, when a woman left the tent for a few minutes, the evangelist interrupted his sermon to explain that she was his wife. He then asked the congregation to pray for her kidney ailment. The following quotation is from a prayer, just before the collection plate was passed one evening at a revival in a small Baptist church in Kentucky.

"Oh God, I pray that you'll bless the giver tonight and the nongiver. Bless any and all. And bless our little daughter who's getting married. And I pray, Lord, that they will be joined together that no man shall asunder them—shall separate them. I thank God that she came to give her heart to God. And this little baby of hers has found its daddy. Oh, Lord God, we take it to Jesus. I'll bet the Lord God has helped this little baby to find its daddy. Lord, she's made a mistake, as many of us have, as we all have. But, God, she's coming back. And this young man has confessed that this is his child, Lord God, tonight. And Lord, when they get married they'll have corrected the wrong that they've done according to the scriptures. And Lord God, tonight I thank you for it.

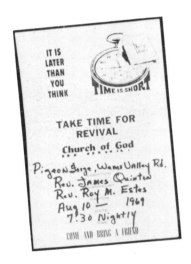

"You've heard our prayers. We've seen our companions shed many tears, and we weep for our children because we love them. And God, we love others tonight. We want to see our children saved tonight. And God bless this offering tonight. Let this be a generous offering in Jesus' name we pray. Let us say Amen. Thank God.''

Whole families come to revivals together, and there are always young children in the church or tent. They were fascinated by the artist at work–this was something new to them—even though they look on calmly while their parents go into trances, fall onto the floor, or speak in tongues. By the end of a long evening service many can be found asleep in the pews or on blankets spread on the ground. **REV. PAPPY GUBE BEAVER** *sings the following verse of a song during one of his sermons:*

> Suppose you could change eyes with God
>   for just one hour,
> And look upon this world and know all its shame.
> Could you accept the great number of excuses
> That's made each Sunday morning
>   when the church bells ring?

come unto me: for of such is the kingdom of

When the trumpet of the Lord shall sound,
    and the time shall be no more,
And the morning breaks eternal, bright and fair:
When the saved of earth shall gather over on the other shore,
    And the roll is called up yonder,
      I'll be there.

What can wash away my stain?
       Nothing but the blood of Jesus;
What can make me whole again?
       Nothing but the blood of Jesus.
Oh, precious is the flow
That makes me white as snow;
No other fount I know,
       Nothing but the blood of Jesus.

Father Abraham, have mercy on me, and send

Jesus on the main line, tell Him what you want,
If you want the Holy Ghost, tell Him what you want,
If you want the Holy Ghost, tell Him what you want,
If you want the Holy Ghost, tell Him what you want,
Tell Him what you want tonight!

17

Lazarus, that he may dip the tip of his finger in

I looked over Jordan, and what did I see?
       Coming for to carry me home,
A band of angels coming after me,
       Coming for to carry me home.
Swing low, sweet chariot,
       Coming for to carry me home.

water, and cool my tongue; for I am tormented

"Well, just suppose that you're the mother of a young baby and your excuse is that the baby would cry and embarrass you in front of the congregation and possibly irritate the preacher.

"Well, just suppose God would see fit to take away that excuse?

"Oh, you might hear a few complaints from those around you, but that baby's cry wouldn't irritate God, not in the least."

Just under the lectern, in the tent or church where a revival is being held, you will probably find the "mourners' bench." It may actually be a bench, or it may be four or five chairs turned to face the congregation. When the "invitation" or "altar call" is given, those who wish to repent of their sins may come forward, kneel before the mourners' bench and pray for forgiveness. As a revival builds to a climax, it becomes important that as many people come forward as possible—to be saved now because it may be their last chance before death or the Judgment. Rev. Pappy Gube Beaver preaches that "we are living in the end times" and that God "may pull the switch on us at any minute." He further exhorts his congregation to come forward with:

"Sure you want to escape hell, don't you? Yes, you do. There'll be no mercy for you there. There'll be no mother or father there to help you. Prayers will not help you in hell. The rich man cried out and says, 'Lord, somebody bring me some water, just to put on the tip of my tongue so that I might get a little ease.' [Luke 16:24] But nobody heard his cry. He said, 'Go down and tell my brothers not to come to this awful place.' The Lord give him senses in hell to talk and warn the false and dying world to not to come to this awful lake of fire.

"You talk about the fire we feel here sometimes. The hot sun. Hell's going to be fifteen hundred times hotter than that! Think about it tonight, children. You're going to die in the charred pits! And the smoke will go on forever.

"Why do you have to go there? You don't have to go there. It's not God's will. God so loved the world that he gave his only begotten son that whosoever love him 'I will in no wise cast out.' Romans 10 tells you to confess the Lord Jesus Christ and believe that God raised him from the dead. Thou shall be saved. You don't have to go to hell. This is your call tonight. This is your call. You've heard the message. You've heard the warning. And it could be your last call.

"I now pray, without any further invitation, that Miss Scruggs will rise from her seat and come forward as the Holy Spirit is in her now. That's right. Right now she'll come here to these little chairs in front of this rostrum. God will do it. Lord, let her come, right now. I know the devil is a-fighting her. I feel the power of Satan. I feel the powers of Satan upon this woman. God loosen her. Loosen her right now, God, and let her come freely. Let her stand on her feet and come forward now . . . .

in this flame. (LUKE 16:24) Repent ye: for the

Just as I am without one plea,
But that Thy blood was shed for me,
And that Thou bidd'st me come to Thee,
O Lamb of God,
I come! I come!

kingdom of heaven is at hand. (MATTHEW 3:2)

"Ashamed to confess Jesus? Down before this whole sinful congregation? He will be ashamed to confess you before the Father in heaven.

"God be on this young man who held his hand up. May he voluntarily come right down. That's right. Just as he is. He's had an opportunity to and I believe, God, that if he'd be honest with his heart, that God is telling him to come this night. Glory hallelujah! People in their automobiles, or wherever they might be, boys and girls, I ask you to get out of your cars and come down to this altar in Jesus' precious name while we sing this invitation song. We pray. Amen."

The song:

> Just as I am, without one plea
> But that thy blood was shed for me,
> And that Thou bidd'st me come to Thee,
> O Lamb of God, I come—I come!

Make a joyful noise unto the Lord, all ye lands.

You ask me why I'm thankful,
   Why I sing and pray and shout:
I found God at the mourners' bench,
   When I began to pray.

Serve the Lord with gladness: come before his

Make a Joyful Noise unto the Lord

Music can always be found at revivals in great quantity and variety. At an urban Baptist church the congregation will sing "Rock of Ages" with dutiful seriousness, while in a tent in a rural area the gentle melody of "Amazing Grace" may be transformed into something resembling hard rock. In churches where the congregations are mostly black, the music often has a softer quality and the hymns sung are those with words of comfort, such as "Come By Here," "Leaning on the Everlasting Arms," or "Peace, Peace, Be Still." Instruments vary with churches and may range from pianos and organs to bass fiddles, tambourines (referred to in the Bible as timbrels), accordions, cymbals, various brasses and woodwinds, banjos, guitars, and a few instruments the artist had never heard before.

REV. PAPPY GUBE BEAVER, *Knoxville, Tennessee:* "We appreciate Sister Forster tonight playing them spoons up here for the glory of God. Well, I—you know, I've found that spoons were made for something besides to eat with. You can make a sound for the Lord—and play a tune with them. Before I played the old guitar—I was raised on the farm and Mother and Daddy wasn't able to buy us a guitar—I used to get the old washtub out and play on it. I'd play and maybe get the broom and make like I was playing the guitar for the glory of God."

Electric guitars are becoming steadily more popular, and now most churches, even small ones, are equipped with amplifying systems. Often the younger members of the congregation collect and save money for the necessary equipment.

JOE TURNER, *Camp Creek, West Virginia:* "I like a mike. A lot of people's scared of them, but I think it helps you. The Bible says, well, to make a joyful noise unto the Lord. I've seen Sister Julie stand right here one night—and she left a sign right here on this Bible stand where she beat it with a tambourine. And about the time I got an aluminium dishpan—and Brother Leonard or some of them brought it here—and I think I pounded the bottom out of it. Why? Do you know what? People slams and throws and cusses and carries on and fights and throws beer bottles and makes about all kind of racket for the devil. Why not do some of it for the Lord? That's what the matter with people today. They've got to think too modern, Brother Jimmy. They don't like this and they don't like that. I think if it takes it to glorify God, you can whap your guitar up against the side of that wall, then let it go. I'll help you buy another one. Glory to God!"

ANOTHER PREACHER *in a small, one-room rural church in Kentucky:* "Some of these people—I don't know—I don't want to say too much,

presence with singing. (PSALM 100:1-2)

52 Life's Railway to Heaven.
(Respectfully dedicated to the railroad men).

M. E. Abbey.
COPYRIGHT, 1891, BY CHARLIE D. TILLMAN.
Charlie D. Tillman.

Solo or Duet. *Tempo ad lib.*
M. 72

1. Life is like a moun-tain rail-road, With an en-gi-neer that's brave;
2. You will roll up grades of tri-al; You will cross the bridge of strife;
3. You will oft-en find ob-struc-tions; Look for storms of wind and rain;
4. As you roll a-cross the tres-tle, Spanning Jor-dan's swell-ing tide,

We must make the run suc-cess-ful, From the cra-dle to the grave;
See that Christ is your con-duc-tor On this light-ning train of life;
On a fill, or curve, or tres-tle, They will al-most ditch your train;
You be-hold the Un-ion De-pot In-to which your train will glide;

Watch the curves, the fills, the tun-nels; Nev-er fal-ter, nev-er quail;
Al-ways mind-ful of ob-struc-tion, Do your du-ty, nev-er fail;
Put your trust a-lone in Je-sus; Nev-er fal-ter, nev-er fail;
There you'll meet the Su-perin-ten-dent, God the Fa-ther, God the Son,

rit.

Keep your hand up-on the throt-tle, And your eye up-on the rail.
Keep your hand up-on the throt-tle, And your eye up-on the rail.
Keep your hand up-on the throt-tle, And your eye up-on the rail.
With the heart-y, joy-ous plaud-it, "Wea-ry pil-grim, wel-come home!"

CHORUS.

Bless-ed Sav-ior, Thou wilt guide us Till we reach that bliss-ful shore;

Where the an-gels wait to join us In Thy praise for-ev-er-more.

24

Make a joyful noise unto the Lord all the earth:

but some of them tonight, some of them don't understand about guitars, you know, and sometimes the music is really not as joyful as it should be. You know, the scripture says a joyful noise. They [*the amplifiers*] are all right if you turn them down to a reasonable level. But in a place this small it bothers me. That's one reason my wife went home. She wasn't feeling too good. You can take guitars and sing with them, you know. It makes a joyful noise and it does—music does a lot for people. And I wouldn't want to say anything to hurt anybody's feelings."

After revival meetings, Eleanor Dickinson did her best to speak to each person she had drawn and ask, "What is your favorite hymn?" Thus she found titles for most of her portraits. Whenever it was impossible to speak to a subject, she titled the drawing with a hymn she had heard that evening or one that she felt was appropriate. Some of the favorites were familiar—there were many duplications—but some were extremely old, and she discovered much church music she had never heard before.

Some of the most interesting hymns have often been written about current events. For instance, it was no easy task to build and maintain railroads over the Appalachian Mountains, but the coming of the railroads made a great difference in people's lives. It was certainly appropriate to compose a hymn about it. When the telephone became common in the area, hymn writers responded with "The Royal Telephone," the text of which tells us that you can talk to God at any time because "Central's never busy." In 1927 when all of the East Tennessee and much of the nation was preoccupied with the Scopes "monkey trial," a number of religious songs appeared on the subject, such as "The Bible Tells Me So." This text of course insists that God created man in the Garden of Eden and "no lower he began." Later, when hymn writers heard about psychology, they produced, "I Don't Want to Get Adjusted to This World," the idea being that there is no point in getting adjusted to the world we live in, since sooner or later we're going to "a home that's so much better." And hymns and gospel songs are still being written. Many of the latter available on records are sung at revival meetings, such as "We Need a Whole Lot More of Jesus and a Lot Less Rock and Roll." One heard occasionally is called "Place Kick Me, Jesus, Through the Goal Posts of Life."

Dickinson has known J. T. Higdon and his sister Midge since she first began to visit her grandparents' summer cabin in the Smoky Mountains as a child. The Higdons have spent most of their lives in Elkmont, Tennessee, and they often went with her to revivals in small mountain churches where any stranger would have been looked upon with suspicion. It was J. T. and Midge Higdon who showed her their family hymnal containing "The Romish Lady." Like many secular ballads found in the area this hymn tells a long and sad story, that of a young

make a loud noise, and rejoice, and sing praise.

No. 54. Are You Washed in the Blood?

E. A. H.   E. A. H.

1. Have you been to Je - sus for the cleans-ing pow'r? Are you
2. Are you walk-ing dai - ly by the Sav-iour's side? Are you
3. When the Bridegroom com - eth, will your robes be white, Pure and
4. Lay a - side the gar-ments that are stained with sin, And be

wash'd in the blood of the Lamb? Are you ful - ly trust-ing in His
wash'd in the blood of the Lamb? Do you rest each mo - ment in the
white in the blood of the Lamb? Will your soul be read - y for the
wash'd in the blood of the Lamb; There's a fount-ain flow - ing for the

CHORUS.

grace this hour? Are you wash'd in the blood of the Lamb?
Cru - ci - fied? Are you wash'd in the blood of the Lamb? } Are you
man-sions bright, Are you wash'd in the blood of the Lamb?
soul un-clean, Are you wash'd in the blood of the Lamb?

wash'd in the blood, In the soul-cleansing blood of the Lamb? Are your
Are you wash'd in the blood,   of the Lamb?

garments spotless? Are they white as snow? Are you wash'd in the blood of the Lamb?

PSALM 100:1 MAKE A JOYFUL NOISE UNTO THE LORD. STRINGED INSTRUMENTS, SINGING. DANCE. TRUMPET. ORGAN, LOUD CYMBALS, FAST. FAST. FAST.

Sing unto the Lord with the harp; with the harp,

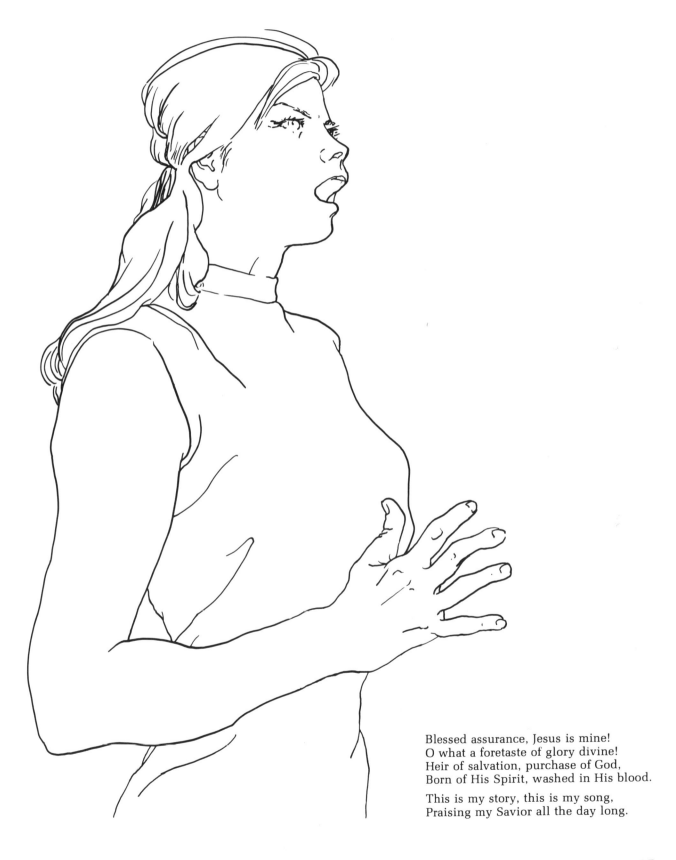

Blessed assurance, Jesus is mine!
O what a foretaste of glory divine!
Heir of salvation, purchase of God,
Born of His Spirit, washed in His blood.

This is my story, this is my song,
Praising my Savior all the day long.

No. 176. THE ROMISH LADY.

Arr. by J. B. V.

1. There was a Rom-ish la - dy bro't up in po-per - y, Her moth-er always
2. As - sisted by her hand-maid her Bible she concealed, And there she gained in-
3. I'll bow to my dear Saviour, and worship God un-seen, I'll live by faith for-
4. With grief and great vexa-tion, her mother straight did go, To inform the Roman
5. The more they strove to fright her, the more she did endure, Altho' her age was
6. Be - fore the Pope they bro't her in hope of her return, But there she was con-
7. There be - ing ma-ny lad - ies assembled at the place, She raised her eyes to
8. Yourselves you need to pit - y, on Zi-on's deep decay, Dear la-dies turn to
9. O take from me these idols, remove them from my sight, Re-store to me my
10. Tor - mentors use your pleasure, do as you think the best, I hope my blessed
11. Instead of golden bracelets, with chains they bound her fast, She cried my God give

taught her the priest she must o-bey; O par - don me, dear moth - er, I
struc-tion till God His love revealed; No more she prostrated her - self to
ev - er, for the works of men are vain; I can not wor-ship an - gels, nor
cler - gy, the cause of all her woe; The priests did soon as-sem - ble and
ten - der, her faith was strong and sure; The chains of gold so cost - ly they
demn - ed in hor-rid flames to burn; Be - fore the place of tor - ment they
heav - en and begged supplying grace; Weep not, ye ten-der la - dies, shed
Je - sus, no long-er make de - lay; In comes her rav-ing moth - er, her
Bi - ble, where-in I take de - light; A - las! my a - ged moth - er, where-
Je - sus will take my soul to rest; Soon as these words were spoken, up
pow - er, now must I die at last? With Je - sus and His an - gels, for-

humbly pray thee now, For un-to these false I - dols I can no long-er bow.
pictures decked with gold, But soon she was betrayed and her Bible from her stole.
pictures made by men. Dear mother use your pleasure, but pardon if you can.
for the maid did call, And forced her in a dungeon to fright her soul with all.
from this la-dy took, And she with all her spir-it the pride of life for-sook.
bro't her speedi - ly With lift-ed hands to heav-en, she then agreed to die.
not one tear for me, While my poor body is burning my soul the Lord shall see.
daughter to be-hold, And in her hand she bro't her pictures decked with gold.
on my ru-in bent, 'Twas you that did be-tray me, and I am in - no-cent.
steps the man of death, And kindled up the fire to stop her mortal breath.
ev - er I shall dwell, God pardon priest and people, and so I bid fare-well.

(109)

28

woman who gave her life for her religious beliefs, which were in opposition to the Roman Catholic Church. The text is thought to have originated in France, although its earliest written form was found in England, dated 1632. It may well have been popular with the early settlers of the southern mountains, many of whom were of Huguenot or Scotch-Irish origin and had come to the New World seeking religious freedom.

In "The Romish Lady" and many early hymns you will find that the notes are often in the shape of triangles, squares, half-circles, and so on. This system of musical notation was popular in New England in the days before the Revolution, when singing masters traveled through the Colonies teaching the musically illiterate settlers to "read," finding a tone by the shape of a note rather than by its position on the staff. In fact, in some early hymnals the notes appear with no staff at all.

Later, as cities along the eastern seaboard grew more sophisticated, the singing masters followed the pioneers to the West and South. Then several systems of "shape-note" singing developed, as new shapes were introduced or the sequence of shapes varied. The diagram below illustrates the system used in the hymns reproduced here. If a hymn is written in the key of F, we can count on the note F appearing as an equilateral triangle and the other shapes following in sequence as shown.

Do   Re   Mi   Fa   Sol   La   Ti   Do

Hymnals are still printed today with shape-notes, partly through tradition but also because the shapes are actually still used by many singing groups in the South. Many people in the revival congregations today, however, do not know the meaning of the shapes. Some think "music just ought to look that way." Others ignore the hymnals completely and sing from memory the songs they have been singing since they were children.

At a time when many people were illiterate or there were no hymnbooks available, a process called "lining out" became popular. This means that the preacher sings a line or phrase of a hymn, then the congregation sings it following his words and melody. Lining out is still used in some churches today.

REV. PAPPY GUBE BEAVER does not read music, but he plays the guitar

Lord, the King. (PSALM 98:4-6)   Praise him

When we all get to heaven,
What a day of rejoicing that will be!
When we all see Jesus,
We'll sing and shout the victory!

by ear and has composed a number of religious songs which he sings in his tent and on his radio program.

"About eight or nine years ago, I guess, in the Solway community, they shot through my tent with a shotgun three times, somebody did. Trying to run me out of the community there, for preaching the gospel. And somebody said, 'You're going to have to leave now.'

"I said, 'No. Ain't no devil's going to make me run.' I said, 'If the Lord tells me to leave, I'll leave. But if it's the devil, you're trying to run a bluff on me.' So we call this our tent song. The title of it is "Our Tent Song.""

Just moved into my little tent today.
Singing and preaching, I'm on my way.
Got the little tent and it weren't no fun.
Ain't no devil going to make me run.

I was in the tent here the other night.
Preaching and praying, it was a sight.
Now one got happy and began to shout.
Good sister got jealous and began to pout.
    (Right in church. Ain't that a shame!)

Yes, we'll be right here till September comes.
We'll be right here and we ain't going to run.
Got the big tent and it weren't no fun.
Ain't enough devils in Knoxville
        to make God's children run.
(Can you say Amen?)

REV. JOE M. MILES *during a revival meeting at the Scott Street Assembly of God, Knoxville, Tennessee:* "Come on, let's everybody stand. We're going to need everybody helping us tonight. Put your hands together and let's clap and sing to glory. Come on. I can stand up here and you can stand back there, and let's worship the Lord. Everybody just clap their hands and let's praise God tonight. You might not have them tomorrow night. You might have a wreck on the way home and have them cut off. And you might never get to clap your hands for God anymore. Let's clap our hands and make a joyful noise unto the Lord."

REV. PAPPY GUBE BEAVER: "Amen. That sounds good. You know, David told us to make a joyful sound unto the Lord. We might be a little different to the Catholic Church. We might be a little different to the Baptist Church. We may be a little different to the Presbyterians. But I believe the Lord said, 'Be what you are,' by the grace of God. Amen. We're going to sing another good song tonight and ask you to stand and shake hands with one another."

the psaltery and harp. (PSALM 150:3)

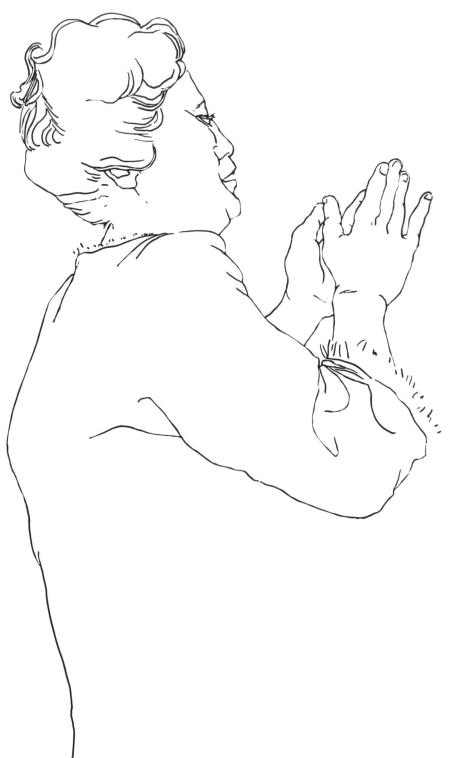

Sing them over again to me,
    Wonderful words of Life;
Let me more of their beauty see,
    Wonderful words of Life,
    Words of life and beauty,
    Teach me faith and duty;
Beautiful words, wonderful words,
    Wonderful words of Life.

Praise him upon the loud cymbals: praise him

When the Saints are marching in
When the Saints are marching in
Joyful songs of salvation thro' the sky shall ring,
When the Saints are marching in.

upon the high sounding cymbals. (PSALM 150:5)

And Miriam the prophetess, the sister of

And David Danced Before the Lord

Revival music, depending upon the denomination, is often accompanied by dancing. Two or more people may dance together. Sometimes one person may dance alone. Groups may gather on the platform to dance, but it is not unusual for others to dance up and down the aisles. Preachers and people in the congregation sometimes hop up and down on one foot as a means of attracting God's attention. **REV. PAPPY GUBE BEAVER** *says that when he is filled with the Holy Ghost and stands on his head, he is doing the holy dance unto the Lord.*

"Amen. If I tried that in the natural spirit, I couldn't make it. But when the Spirit of God is upon me, Brother Smith, you can get around. Cause he gets you around. Amen. Thank God. I believe in doing the holy dance for the Lord, don't you? Amen. Praise the Lord."

ELZIE PREAST *explains:* "It's kindly like a man I know said about his wife. He said, 'I know that had to be the Lord on her—when she danced and had a big time in the Lord.' He said, 'I know that had to be the Lord on her because she's too lazy to do that in herself.'"

REV. ROGER POWELL, *pastor of the Church of God of the Mountain Assembly in Lake City, Tennessee, taught himself to read from the King James version of the Bible. The following is from one of the religious pamphlets he now writes and distributes. First Reverend Powell lists the scriptural references he has collected which refer to dancing:*

And Miriam the prophetess, the sister of Aaron, took a timbrel in her hand; and all the women went out after her with timbrels and with dances. (EXODUS 15:20)

Let them praise his name in the dance. . . . (PSALM 149:3)

Praise him with the timbrel and dance. . . . (PSALM 150:4)

And David danced before the Lord with all his might. . . .
(II SAMUEL 6:14)

"You know, all the emotions of praises unto the Lord have been taken over by the devil and used for merchandise. Now I believe those women that danced did it because they were happy and felt their security from the hand of the devil. And I believe those beautiful saints of God looked like Holiness people; they looked like God made them. I would guarantee that they had no makeup on, no fingernail polish, no diamonds, and I would love to have seen their beautiful long hair, and them fully dressed, dancing for the glory of God because they had won the victory. I love to see people dance under the power of the Spirit of God. When you are filled with the Spirit, you're filled with joy and you have got to do something about it. You have got to shout, dance, run, clap your

Aaron, took a timbrel in her hand; and all the

I've wandered far away from God,
   Now I'm coming home;
The paths of sin too long I've trod,
   Lord, I'm coming home.
Coming home, coming home, never more to roam;
Open wide Thine arms of Love,
   Lord, I'm coming home.

women went out after her with timbrels and

We'll be like Him,
We'll be like Him,
We'll be like Him, some day;
O deep in my heart
I do believe
We'll be like Him, some day.

with dances. (EXODUS 15:20)   Let them praise

Great God, what do I see and hear!
    The end of things created!
The Judge of all men doth appear,
    On clouds of glory seated:
The trumpet sounds; the graves restore
    The dead which they contained before;
Prepare, my soul, to meet him.

his name in the dance... (PSALM 149:3)

hands, cry out to God with a loud voice and make a joyful noise unto him. Praise him for his mighty acts; praise him with the sound of the trumpet, upon the high-sounding cymbals.

"You can snap the rein of a horse to a hitching post and he will stand there, because he knows he is tied. Then you walk up and unsnap the rein and he will stand still until he discovers he is loose. So it is with the man or woman today. They let other people blindfold them until they cannot see the great fields of clover God has led them out in. They do not know of the gifts that Christ has given his ministers for their benefit. Christ rejoiced in the spirit. So you should go forward and claim the victory in Christ, and the love of God will take over in your heart, soul, mind, and body; then you will dance for the glory of God."

JOE TURNER, *Camp Creek, West Virginia:* "I've seen people that have the Holy Ghost, maybe some of them would dance right on that cord, the guitar cord or mike cord. Somebody else who used it didn't have enough sense to move it over. Just let them dance right on top of it. Well, it's God's cord. Won't hurt you to move it. Them things is very costly. I couldn't explain the money I've spent for it. Well, seems like that's just as holy as anything else. Take care of it.

"Some people said they come to Camp Creek Church and that 'all they want to do is dance, dance, dance.' Well, if you needed gasoline, would you go to a liquor store to get it? No, you'd go to a filling station, or somebody's tank beside of the road. Thank God. Yeah, thank God! If you want to dance, then go to the house of God. The Bible says, 'Fail not to assemble yourselves together.' All right. Thank God. You know what? The more they talk about me dancing, the more I dance. I don't know why God just puts it on me to go right on. Sometimes I get in a service, about the second time they hit that guitar there, something starts moving in my legs and feet. Makes me want to get right out on the floor and begin to dance. Now it doesn't matter to me too much what you think about me. Now if you think there's no God in that at all, I'm going to dance right on. I'm going to dance right on. Praise God! The Bible said, 'Praise him with the dance.' Why not dance? Thank God, thank God. I dance a lot, Brother Preast. I get the girls sometimes—or whoever I can get ahold of—and into a dance we go."

Joe Turner on another evening: "Sometimes when I go to church, people say, 'Well, what's the matter with Brother Turner?' Now I went down to church last night. And for all of the dancing and singing and playing music—and I was a-setting there saying, 'Lord, let me discern out this and let me feel this and let me feel that.' It's wonderful sometimes, Brother Preast—Amen—just to sit down and ask God to let me feel the thing that's necessary tonight. Amen. There's more to it than just dancing and hollering, ain't there? And I like to do both of them. Hallelujah! So when you pray, please remember me."

And David danced before the Lord with all his

Give me that old time religion,
Give me that old time religion,
Give me that old time religion
It's good enough for me!

might...(II SAMUEL 6:14) Praise ye the Lord.

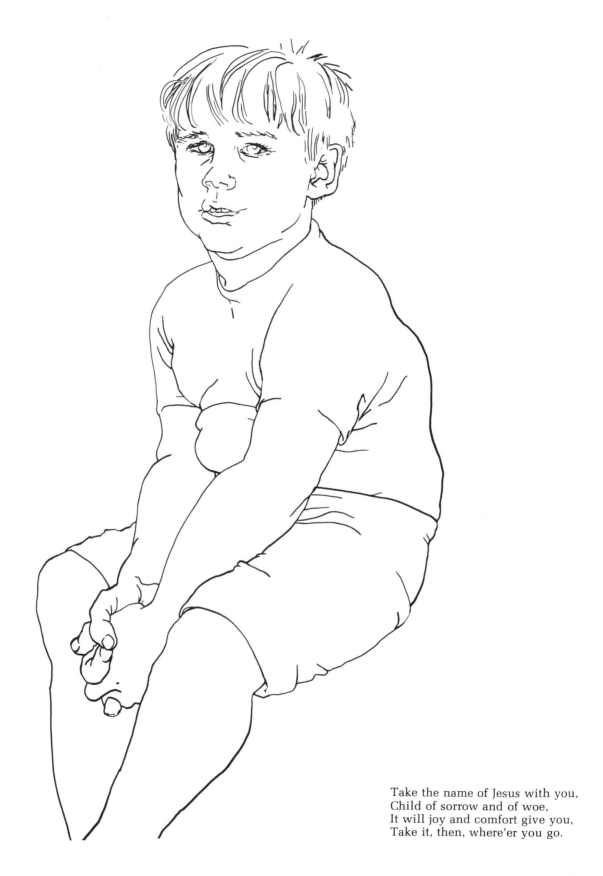

Take the name of Jesus with you,
Child of sorrow and of woe,
It will joy and comfort give you,
Take it, then, where'er you go.

Sing unto the Lord a new song, and his praise

If you're talking about the old time religion,
  Then I know what you're talking about.
About the kind that will make you love your neighbor,
  When old Satan says "Turn him out!"

in the congregation of saints. (PSALM 149:1)

Stand Up and Testify

It is not only the evangelist who speaks at a revival. Any member of the congregation may stand and testify. Usually those testifying bear witness to what God has done in their lives. They may speak calmly and quietly, or they may shout. Sometimes they cry.

ELZIE PREAST, *Scrabble Creek, West Virginia:* "Somebody get up and testify. Get up and tell how you feel tonight. Maybe you're disgusted and worried or you're mad at somebody. If you get up and tell it, it'd probably do you good to get it off your stomach. It's sour stuff that will stay and get worse all the time—mold over."

REV. JOE M. MILES, *Knoxville, Tennessee:* "Sister Quentin, stand up and shout a little bit."

SISTER QUENTIN: "I can't shout. But I'm always willing to stand up and say that I know that my Redeemer liveth—glory hallelujah! I'm glad that I've been redeemed by the blood of the Lamb. I'm glad that I know that my sins are under the blood."

Wear Valley is a green and fertile area in the heart of the Smoky Mountains. It is filled with small neat farms, and many churches. Here the pastor of a church is often a farmer who plows his own fields during the week and preaches on Sundays. A woman called **SISTER GIVENS** *is active in a small church in Wear Valley. She leads singing and works among young people in the congregation. One revival meeting began with her testimony.*

"Praise God! You talk about the living God. Well, people of the world just can't understand because they've got the spirit of the world. And they can't get being born again in the kingdom of God. And they say they can't understand sometimes why people jump and holler and say, 'I praise the Lord!' or 'I glorify the Lord!' And when people say things like that to me, I just look right back at them there and grin. Well, I hope God gets glory out of some of them, the way they act sometimes. But I'm afraid he's not. Cause we're going to have to praise him with everything that we've got. With all of our minds and all of our hearts and all of our spirit. You know, God don't want a halfway living creature, but he's wanting one that's going to live for him always.

"This world ain't got nothing for me. If it did, I'd get out in the world. But these places never done a thing for me. People look at me and say, 'Why, you're not doing nothing. You're not having no fun at all.' I was working at this place in Morristown, and people were always coming in talking about parties they'd been going to on the weekend. And how they'd get drunk and how they'd danced and everything. And they'd look at me and say, 'Don't you ever do nothing?'

We speak that we do know, and testify that

My Lord, what a morning,
My Lord, what a morning,
My Lord, what a morning
When the stars begin to fall.

"I said, 'Yes.' I said, 'I go to church.' I said, 'I go about every night the church door is open.' And I said, 'On Sunday I go twice—and sometimes three times if I can find an evening service somewhere.'

"They looked at me, and they'd say, 'Well—ain't you ever had no fun before in your life? Ain't you ever been to a party?'

"I said, 'No, not the kind you're talking about.' I said, 'I never did really want to go. And my daddy wouldn't have let me if I'd wanted to. And I thank God for him.' Said, 'When I got something within my heart, when Jesus began to live within my heart—he came in one night in a little Baptist mission when I gave my heart to God—well, I didn't have no more wants or any more worries about the world because that's all left behind. I don't want anything else to do with it because I got Jesus. And he lives within my heart.'

"People thinking about the spirit of the world, the reason why that they can't really get in with us is that they don't understand. I tell them about Jesus and they just look at me like they don't know what I'm talking about. Jesus ain't understood in the spirit of the world, and they ain't yet give their hearts to God. And they're still in darkness, and they don't understand. A lot of times we'll say, 'Well, it just seems like we've got to shake it into them.' Why, shaking it into somebody's not going to do any good at all. We've got to give it to them in love. We've got to give it to them through the word of God. And oh, there's nothing like serving the Lord. I do praise him."

A man called **BROTHER OWENS** *was brought in a wheel chair to a revival at a tent north of Knoxville, Tennessee.* **THE PREACHER** *told the congregation,* "I want Brother Owens to say a word or two. My, he's been through a lot, but he don't want no pity. He just keeps going for the Lord. Say what you want to, Brother Owens."

"Thank you, Brother Logan. It's good to be in the house of God today. And most of all, it's good to feel that I'm in a position that you can feel the goodness of God. Now people might look on me and feel sorry for me and all those things. But I don't want your pity. And I don't want you to feel sorry for me because—thank God—back yonder eighteen years ago that something-or-another come into my heart and I haven't got over it since. And, thank God, I don't think I ever will get over it. I dread to die. And I dread a lot of things. But thank God I don't fear them. We've got the Son of God in our hearts that'll lead us and guide us. I'm thankful for the Book of Job—there where Job told all the suffering and things that he went through. And he said that all his friends come and told him he was a hypocrite and he was backslid and he'd done this and he'd done that. And old Job, he got down and said, 'Lord, there's two things that I desire that you not let happen unto me. Just not to cause my dread to become fear. And not withdraw your hand far from me.'

"If I should pray God for anything today, above everything else then

would praise the Lord for his goodness, and

O I can never forget how the fire fell,
When the Lord sanctified me.

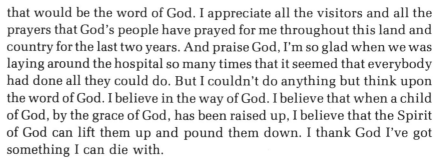

that would be the word of God. I appreciate all the visitors and all the prayers that God's people have prayed for me throughout this land and country for the last two years. And praise God, I'm so glad when we was laying around the hospital so many times that it seemed that everybody had done all they could do. But I couldn't do anything but think upon the word of God. I believe in the way of God. I believe that when a child of God, by the grace of God, has been raised up, I believe that the Spirit of God can lift them up and pound them down. I thank God I've got something I can die with.

"Thank God, I can't find in the word of God nowhere that it says that we're going to have all the things in this life. But, thank God, one thing that God promised us, that we could have a home in heaven and it would be eternal. I don't know what I'll have to go through from here on out, but I know one thing. That the Son of God's come with me this far, and I believe he'll go with me all the way. Thank God. I thank God for the afflictions that we have in this body. I know many people that's been saved—they say they've been saved—and their head's down. And it seems like that everything's going wrong. But praise God, the word of God says for us to look up and to rejoice because we know that our redemption draweth nigh. We can look around at the things that are happening in this world. And I believe that I shall not look down. That our redemption draweth nigh. It's good to be here. Thank you, Brother Logan. Lead us in prayer."

The following testimony is by **A WOMAN**—*also in a wheel chair—at Rev. Pappy Gube Beaver's tent. As she spoke, her voice rose to a hysterical pitch.*

"I want to tell you all that this man [*Reverend Beaver*] has been wonderful to me. I'll tell you. I was back in sin. And I came back to the Lord and he has blessed me all the way. And I want you all to keep praying. My daughter is coming home by his prayers. And God can help and I know. My sister over there brought me down in this wheel chair. She said, 'I'm not going into that tent.' She said, 'I'm going to sit out here in the car and let you go in.' But there were so many prayers going up for her that she had to come into the tent that night. God bless this man. Protect him, dear God, and help him. Oh, dear Jesus! This is a wonderful time, O Lord. Oh thank you, God, for everything you've done for me, dear Jesus! Oh, dear Jesus, thank you, dear Lord! Protect this poor man and help him, dear Lord. He's going to help everybody he can, dear God. Please be with him. Give him the strength to do what he needs to do, dear God.

"They told me this afternoon they would send my daughter home to me, dear God. Oh, Jesus, I'm so happy for this, dear God. Thank you, Jesus! Oh they said they had money there. And they'd send her home by bus. I could pick her up at the bus, dear God. Oh thank you, dear Jesus,

men! (PSALM 107:8)   O give thanks unto the

O love that will not let me go
I rest my weary soul in thee:
I give thee back the life I owe
That in thine ocean depths its flow
May richer, fuller be.

Lord; call upon his name: make known his

for everything, dear God, that you have meant to me. Lord, if I hadn't a come back to you when I did, dear God, I'd a never got my daughter back. I know that, dear God. Bless you, Jesus, for everything, dear Lord. Oh, Jesus, help my poor sister, dear God. Help her in all her sufferings and needs. Please help her! She's having trouble, dear Lord. Please help her, God! Oh, give her the strength to go on doing what she needs to do. Oh, thank you, dear Jesus. . . ."

ANOTHER WOMAN *at Rev. Pappy Gube Beaver's tent:* "I want to thank the Lord for being here tonight. I want to thank him for all he's done for me. He's healed my body many times. And he's healed my baby. And I thank him for saving my soul.

"You know, I believe the last time we was over here, along last summer, we had an awful good service. You know, I'm glad I can stand up for the Lord. This Sunday religion may be all right if you die on Sunday. But you know, there's six more days in the week that you can die on besides Sunday. So you better live it seven days a week, not just Sunday. I don't believe in just a Sunday religion."

deeds among the people. (PSALM 105:1)

O happy day, that fixed my choice
   On Thee, my Savior and my God!
      Happy day, happy day,
        When Jesus washed my sins away.

And when the day of Pentecost was fully come,

Pentecostalism and the Holy Ghost

Many of the revivals Eleanor Dickinson visited were sponsored by churches that can be described as Pentecostal, such as Holiness, Church of God, Assembly of God, and others. The name Pentecostal comes from Pentecost, the fiftieth day from the resurrection of Christ, when according to the Book of Acts, chapter 2, the twelve apostles gathered together as they had been instructed to do. It was at this time that tongues of flame were seen to rest upon each of them, and thus they received the baptism of the Holy Ghost by fire. It is said that they began to speak "with other tongues" and henceforth were able to perform miracles. It is the firm belief of the Pentecostals that it is still possible to receive the baptism of the Holy Ghost, or Holy Spirit, making God a very real force in their daily lives. They believe that when they are filled with the Spirit they can do many things they could not do "in the natural." [I Corinthians 2:14.] For instance Mrs. Foster, a native of East Tennessee, believes that the Holy Ghost has given her the power to paint religious pictures. She has had no art training and uses simple materials, usually pens and colored crayons. Some examples of her work are reproduced in this chapter.

Most Pentecostals feel that other denominations, although they may profess belief in the Trinity, do not put enough emphasis on the Holy Ghost.

REV. PAPPY GUBE BEAVER, *Knoxville, Tennessee:* "Why is it people want to leave the Holy Ghost and the fire out of it—and all the other Nine Gifts of God. It's all in there. There's Nine Gifts in the Book of Corinthians. It's part of everyone tonight, Brother Lepner. Thank God, we'd just as well—we take part of the Bible, why not take it all? I'd rather be where the full gospel is being preached, Sister. I believe in God's saving power. I believe in God's divine healing—can you say Amen?

"You know, in the world today, that sometimes they have these people that come after you—the yippies or hippies they call them —with the *new* Jesus movement on them. And they're pitching all kinds of fits and letting their hair grow down their back. Why, honey, there's nothing new in the movement of Jesus. That happened back yonder at Calvary—hallelujah—almost two thousand years ago. Healing has always been. The Holy Ghost has been. The Gifts has always been. It's been the people that is too stubborn to believe them. Come on, say Amen."

Not only are the Pentecostals the fastest-growing group of Christians in the world today, but there are elements of Pentecostalism appearing in other faiths—Protestant, Catholic, and Jewish. The Pentecostal

they were all with one accord in one place. And

suddenly there came a sound from heaven as of

movement is sometimes referred to as "charismatic," from the Greek word charisma *meaning gift. The Nine Gifts Pappy Beaver refers to are the gifts of the Holy Ghost listed by the Apostle Paul in his first epistle to the Corinthians, chapter 12:*

Wisdom	*Prophecy*
Knowledge	*Discerning of spirits*
Faith	*Speaking in divers tongues*
Healing	*Interpretation of tongues*
Working of miracles	

A PREACHER in Wear Valley, Tennessee, tells his revival congregation: "If you don't have the miracle of the Nine Gifts operating in this church, don't you blame this district church down here. But just blame yourself—glory to God. If you'll get down on your knees and pray and fast and seek God, the Lord will let the miracles work through me and be operating in the church—in this church. Amen. Don't blame that on me. That's what sayeth the word of God.

"If you're saved, you're an instrument of God tonight. If you're sanctified, you're an altar of God tonight. If you're filled with the Holy Ghost, with the evidence of speaking in tongues, you have the Comforter. You have the abiding Spirit within you. The Lord will stand and help you to be an overcomer when the devil comes your way and tries to smite at each chance. You've got the third person in the Godhead to stand up and war with you. Do you know, the Bible says, 'Put on the whole armor of God.' It didn't mean natural weapons, but it meant spiritual weapons—glory to God. The word of God says to be wise as a serpent but harmless as a dove—glory to God. That means to stay still and let God fight your battles for you. That means be in the way of God at all times."

REV. PAPPY GUBE BEAVER: "If you get glorified with the Holy Ghost, it's a leader. It's a keeper and will keep you in these evil times when the devil is coming with all his evil powers. I tell you, God will—I tell you, God will hold you in the time of all the persecution. The Holy Ghost will keep you. It's a preserver. My mother used to can fruit. You know, like canned berries and—well—kill a hog and can the sausage. And she'd always clean them cans out good, you know, and she put a preserving powder in that fruit to keep it, you know. And they'd have to be airtight. Well, that's the way of the Holy Ghost. Thank God. It's a preserver, and it keeps us preserved in the love of God—Amen—when the devil begins to raise."

JOE TURNER: "Now the devil will tell you tonight, you're all right just like you are. Ah, but brother, listen. Jesus said unto Nicodemus, 'You must be borned again.' Ah, brother, listen. Ah, glory to God, when Jesus cried, 'I've come into this old boy's soul,' I passed out of this world. I didn't know I was in it. And when I come to myself, I was on the floor a-preaching the gospel to other people and telling them about the great experience that I'd had. Amen. I shouted and spoke in tongues for about two hours. Ah, glory to God.''

Speaking in tongues, also known as glossolalia, is one of the Nine Gifts often encountered at revivals and always considered as a sign that a person has received the baptism of the Holy Ghost, although St. Paul in his first letter to the Corinthians warns that it should not be given undue importance. Often a preacher will speak a few sentences in tongues several times during a sermon. Sometimes a man or woman in the congregation will stand and spontaneously begin a long speech in tongues. Another may rise and interpret—the gift of interpretation of tongues. The interpretation is usually in a King James, Biblical kind of English. It may be a prayer or it may be spoken in the first person, indicating the gift of prophecy: that God is speaking through the person filled with the Holy Ghost.

Some feel that the sound of speaking in tongues is similar to that of a Romance language. Others suggest that it is more like Hebrew, an African dialect, ancient Arabic, and so on. The sound in fact varies with different people and in different areas. Much research has been done on the subject, and most agree that glossolalia is not simply gibberish but does have the rhythm and cadence of a language. Tongues can be heard, incidentally, on many Pentecostal radio programs.

JOE TURNER: ''There's something that talks out of the people of God. The world don't know anything about it. It just automatically comes. Why, somebody was telling, Brother Delbert—what language was it that they said I spoke in? Why, listen. I don't know any other language—glory to God—I don't know of any foreign languages of any kind, Brother Preast. Don't know a thing about them. Glory to God. Amen! But I know one thing tonight—praise God—that Jesus holds the reins of my heart. Amen. And when he speaks out, it doesn't matter to me what people says about it. It doesn't matter to me what they call it—glory to God. I'm a-talking about myself because Jesus will talk out of his people—glory to God—and if you've never heard him talk out of you tonight—if you haven't got him yet—glory to God—he's always proved himself everywhere he's been. Hallelujah! Oh, praise God. He speaks for himself tonight when he comes in. And if he quits talking, it sounds like you shut him off somewhere.''

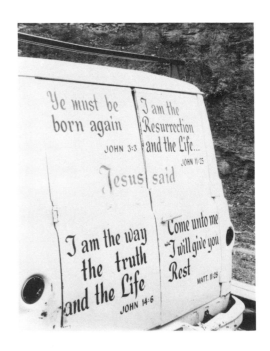

The Book of Acts also states that when the apostles received the baptism of the Holy Ghost and began speaking in tongues, "others mocking said, These men are full of new wine." Members of Pentecostal sects are still "mocked" today. Many have earned the derogatory

house where they were sitting. And there

O how I love Jesus,
O how I love Jesus,
O how I love Jesus,
    Because He first loved me.

appeared unto them cloven tongues like as of fire,

Oh! do not let the Word depart,
    And close thine eyes against the light;
Poor sinner, harden not thy heart:
    Thou would'st be saved—
    Why not tonight?

and it sat upon each of them. And they were all

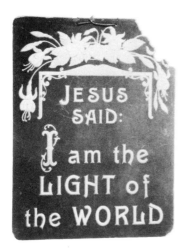

name of Holy Rollers because of their convulsive jerking, dancing, and actual rolling on the floor. **REV. PAPPY GUBE BEAVER** *is known for his enthusiasm while preaching, and when he gets really wound up he will stand on his head or climb a tent pole. According to his wife, "He had an operation last summer but that didn't stop him from standing on his head when the Holy Spirit was on him."*

"I'm called a Holy Roller, and I'm glad of that name, too. I'd rather roll into heaven than to rust out and go to hell, wouldn't you? The Bible said without holiness no man shall see the Lord. Hallelujah! I'm glad tonight it's the Holy Bible from Genesis to Revelations. Well, glory to God, it's a Bible that was written by men that was moved up and filled with the Holy Ghost. Moved up by the power of the Holy Ghost. Can you say Amen?

"I tell you I feel like climbing old Sunshine Mountain—Lord have mercy! Somebody here the other night said, 'Last time I seen Pappy he looked like a squirrel.' I was plumb up there on that pole. I believe I'd have broke my neck if I'd tried that in the natural—in the natural way—in the natural body, you know. But I was carried away in the Holy Spirit.

"My son said, 'Daddy, how'd you get up there on that big thing without a ladder?'

"I said, 'God put me up there.' Amen."

Anyone who receives the gift of prophecy will speak in the first person as if God were actually speaking. The following example is from a revival in a Church of God near Sunset Gap, Tennessee. In this case **THE EVANGELIST,** *while in a trancelike state, allows God to speak through him in English.*

"You listen to the voice of the Lord as he speaks to you tonight. You let him speak to your heart. He understands your needs. He knows your problems. My God knows your problems. God is speaking tonight to this congregation. I feel that there's about five people here tonight that are distressed. But God is speaking to you tonight, saying, 'Fear not my child. Trust in me. I know what I can do. Did I not deliver the children of Israel out of Egypt? Did I not lead them through the Red Sea? Did I not take care of them for forty years in the wilderness? Did I not bring them into that land that flowed with milk and honey? Oh, am I not the God that healed the leper? Am I not the God that raised the dead? Am I not the God that turned the water into wine? Ye that remain, trust in me. For I am the God of all blessings. Is there anything too hard for me? My people, be not weary. Continue to strive. Continue to fight the good fight with me. And have faith in me. And I will show you things to come. And I will be your God. And I will perform miracles among you. Be ye not discouraged, all ye that believe in me. Be thou courageous.

filled with the Holy Ghost, and began to speak

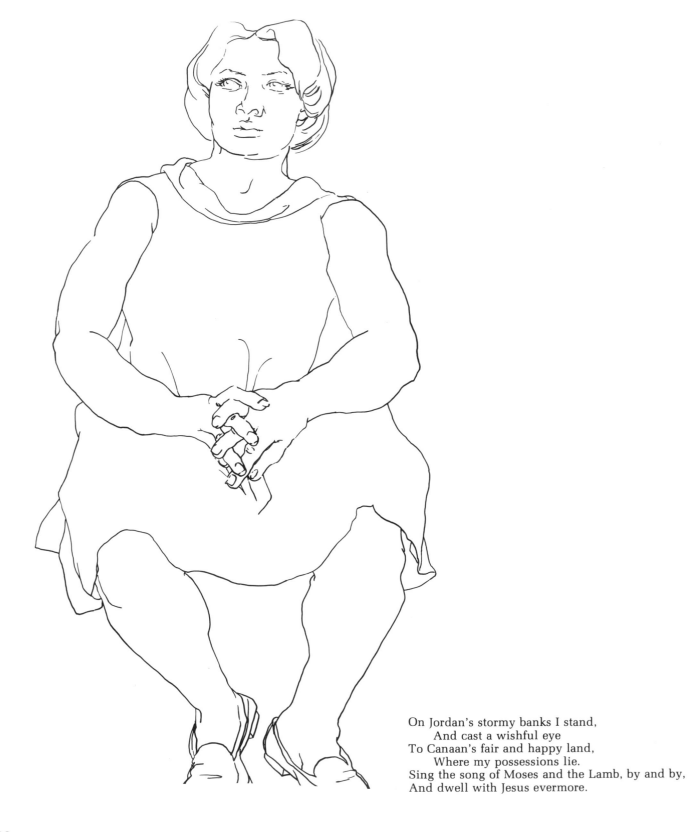

On Jordan's stormy banks I stand,
    And cast a wishful eye
To Canaan's fair and happy land,
    Where my possessions lie.
Sing the song of Moses and the Lamb, by and by,
And dwell with Jesus evermore.

with other tongues, as the Spirit gave them

Sowing in the morning, sowing in the noon-tide and the dewy eve;
Waiting for the harvest, and the time of reaping,
We shall come, rejoicing, bringing in the sheaves.

utterance. (ACTS 2:1-4)   **I indeed baptize you**

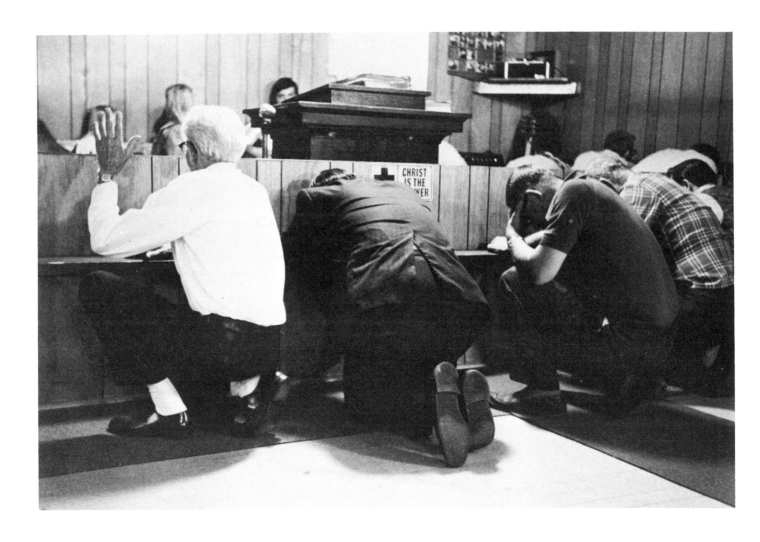

I indeed baptize you

with water unto repentance: but he that cometh

You're my child, and I'm your father. I purchased you, and I bought you with the blood of my son. And do you think I would allow your enemy to overcome you? Behold, I am the captain of your salvation. And I will fight your battle. The battle is not yours. But the battle is mine. Be encouraged, my people. Seek my face. Pray more. And I will bless you. And tomorrow the sun will shine. For it is dark and cloudy and dreary.'

"Hallelujah! Oh, hallelujah! Hallelujah! *(Here the preacher begins to weep.)* Hallelujah—my God, my God, we thank him tonight. I feel that God has spoke to us through prophecy tonight. And I feel that bunch of people that are in need right now. And I want us to sing, 'My God Can Do Anything.' And I want you to listen to the voice of the Lord tonight as he has spoke to us. And put your trust in him. And say, 'I believe you, God. I believe you, God. I believe that you can do anything.' If you believe, come and stand before the altar and sing, 'My God Can Do Anything.' "

Pentecostals believe in baptism with water as well as baptism of the Holy Spirit. Baptism is often referred to as being born again. **REV. ROGER POWELL** *of Lake City, Tennessee, discusses this phenomenon in one of his religious pamphlets. First he quotes from the gospel of John, the third chapter:* "Nicodemus saith unto him, How can a man be born when he is old? Can he enter the second time into his mother's womb, and be born? Jesus answered, Verily, verily, I say unto thee, Except a man be born of water and of the Spirit, he cannot enter into the kingdom of God."

Powell continues, "For a child to be born, the 'water' breaks first —then it comes forth flesh and blood. At this time breath is breathed into it and it becomes a living soul. When Christ was on the cross he had a broken heart and they pierced him in the side and out flowed blood and water. The blood for a covering, the water for a cleanser.

"Now a broken heart will weep and mourn as a mother for her only son. When I preach to sinners and break their hearts, they will cry like a new born baby. The water must break first and if a man will only weep, pray and cry his way through to God in humble repentance, he will be born again."

after me is mightier than I, whose shoes I am

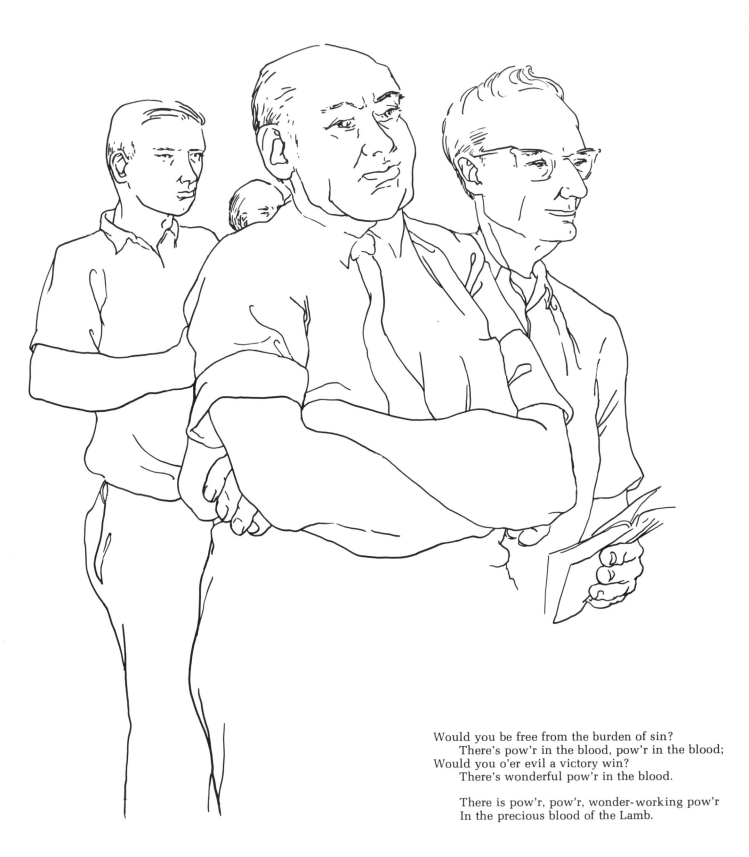

Would you be free from the burden of sin?
    There's pow'r in the blood, pow'r in the blood;
Would you o'er evil a victory win?
    There's wonderful pow'r in the blood.

There is pow'r, pow'r, wonder-working pow'r
In the precious blood of the Lamb.

not worthy to bear: he shall baptize you with

Baptism by Water

If a revival is held in a tent or a small rural church, a baptismal service will quite likely take place in a nearby creek or river. Eleanor Dickinson attended Rev. Pappy Gube Beaver's baptism in Beaver Creek at Dry Gap, near Knoxville, Tennessee, and a joint baptism by the preachers Joe Turner, Elzie Preast, and Robert Washington in the Gauley River near Brownsville, West Virginia. On both occasions she found drawing impossible, but, carrying her camera, she waded into the water along with the candidates for baptism.

At the baptism in the Gauley River, Elzie Preast led the singing while **JOE TURNER** spoke first. "Well, I'd just like to say that I thank the Lord for this day that we're gathered here. And you that are going to be baptized, you're taking a great step. To me it's a great step in the Lord, Brother Charley. And it pays to count the cost of the thing. As Brother Washington mentioned a while ago, when we go out here in this water and take on the name of Jesus today—when we come out of there, let's walk right. Regardless. Let's don't maybe have the thing in the future to redo over again. I feel encouraged—glory to God—that there's people that's willing to go out into the water to make a great change for Jesus. Amen. It says, 'Except you are born of water and of the Spirit'—glory to God—you cannot—Amen—even see into the kingdom of God. Brother Charley, listen. One day you and I must have hid in a womb, glory to God. We come forth—hallelujah—as the world seemed to open up, we come forth as babes—glory to God—Amen. Brother, when we come out of that water, we're born, glory to God. Hallelujah!

"You can't stand beside of somebody like I'm a-standing and baptize people. You got to get ready for baptizing. Let us lift our hands and pray. Jesus, again, Lord as we come before you, you're real—glory to God—and we thank you, Lord, for this hour. We know that thou art a God that faileth not. Lord, you've got all power. You're the same God that spoke unto the sea. Praise God. You're the same God that delivered Daniel from the den of lions. You're the God that's able to move upon every soul that's here in the sound of my voice, Lord, in this hour."

ELZIE PREAST: "I don't know that I have a lot to say, but this is one of the ways to prove that you believe. Just go ahead and do it and the scripture teaches us that we do in the Word, and this is one of the ways you do it, and this is one of the commandments we're keeping. So be assured that you're obeying God with this commandment, because it said to repent and be baptized in the name of Jesus Christ for the remission of sins, and it said you shall receive the gift of the Holy Ghost. Now you that have the Holy Ghost, then this is a necessary thing, too. So just feel that you're obeying the commandment and feel encouraged. Bless every one of you.

the Holy Ghost and with fire . (MATTHEW 3:11)

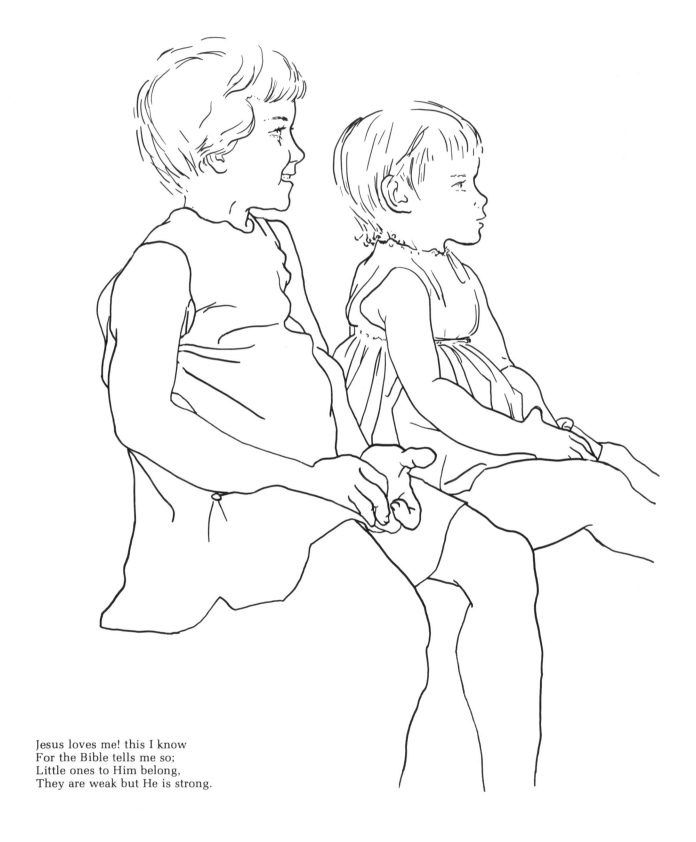

Jesus loves me! this I know
For the Bible tells me so;
Little ones to Him belong,
They are weak but He is strong.

Verily, verily, I say unto thee, Except a man be

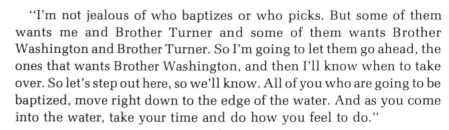

"I'm not jealous of who baptizes or who picks. But some of them wants me and Brother Turner and some of them wants Brother Washington and Brother Turner. So I'm going to let them go ahead, the ones that wants Brother Washington, and then I'll know when to take over. So let's step out here, so we'll know. All of you who are going to be baptized, move right down to the edge of the water. And as you come into the water, take your time and do how you feel to do."

REV. PAPPY GUBE BEAVER *baptized eleven people on a Sunday afternoon at Beaver Creek. When he speaks of the "watery grave" he is referring to the belief that one must symbolically die before being born again.*

"Now you know, when you go down into this watery grave, you'll never forget this day right on this little creek. It'll do something to you. It's not a saving process, but, thank God, it'll be such a blessing when you get in that water. You'll feel the Holy Ghost, Brother Travis. You'll feel the power of God. We've been here before. We've prayed here at this place. Yes, it's an anointing ground. We've got Brother Craig with us—Reverend Craig. If he'd like to say a few words before we sing another song, go ahead and testify. Say something, Brother Craig."

REVEREND CRAIG: "I thank the Lord for this gathering out here. I thank the Lord. I teach baptism as a means of salvation. Jesus said, 'Repent and be baptized and you shall be saved.' I mean, that's the word of God. I hope and pray that every one of you that's never been baptized —Amen—will be baptized today. If there's any in the sound of my voice that might make up their mind, today's the day, man, that you need to step into the water and be baptized, because you may not have an opportunity if you wait a little bit later."

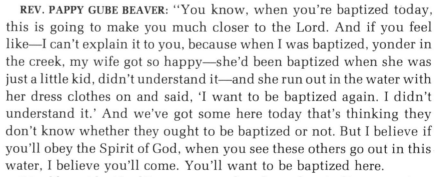

REV. PAPPY GUBE BEAVER: "You know, when you're baptized today, this is going to make you much closer to the Lord. And if you feel like—I can't explain it to you, because when I was baptized, yonder in the creek, my wife got so happy—she'd been baptized when she was just a little kid, didn't understand it—and she run out in the water with her dress clothes on and said, 'I want to be baptized again. I didn't understand it.' And we've got some here today that's thinking they don't know whether they ought to be baptized or not. But I believe if you'll obey the Spirit of God, when you see these others go out in this water, I believe you'll come. You'll want to be baptized here.

"And he said—'And Jesus came and spake to them'—listen, 'saying, All power is given unto me in heaven and in earth.' He said, 'Go ye therefore, and teach all nations, baptizing them in the name of the Father, and of the Son, and of the Holy Ghost: Teaching them to observe all things whatsoever I have commanded you: and, lo, I am with you

born of water and of the Spirit, he cannot enter

always, even unto the end of the world.' Now that's the scriptures. I'll lay the Bible down. That's it. Baptize them in the name of the Father and the Son and the Holy Ghost. And teach them. You know, when Jesus went down to the River Jordan there and he met John the Baptist. And he was baptized there, and the Holy Ghost came down in the form of a dove and lit upon his shoulder and said, 'This is my beloved son who I am well pleased with. Here ye him this day.' When Jesus was baptized, he intended for his children to follow the same examples that he did. That's what he left down here—this is the road map. And this is the thing we should follow. Hallelujah!"

REVEREND CRAIG: "Our father, we come before thee, gathered to see these candidates go into the water. We pray, O God, that thy blessing will rest upon them, Father, that they might grow stronger. Bless the baptizer. Bless Brother Beaver, O God, when he goes to baptize these people, that he might be an example—hallelujah—to all of us."

REVEREND BEAVER: "We want everybody to sing this old song and listen to the words to it. Thank God we have Sister Kent here. She's willing to help us here. But I know many of you can sing the chorus. 'Shall We Gather at the River?' You know this will bring back—this will put something in your mind and heart—Jesus when he was baptized there, and when there were many baptized in the River of Jordan."

> Shall we gather at the river,
> Where bright angel feet have trod;
> With its crystal tide forever
> Flowing by the throne of God?
>
> Yes, we'll gather at the river,
> The beautiful, the beautiful river,
> Gather with the saints at the river
> That flows by the throne of God.

"I can tell you I feel something in that old song, Brother Craig. 'Shall We Gather at the River?' All right. Get your shouting shoes on cause it's time. Amen."

While the others continued singing on the bank, the candidates for baptism descended into Beaver Creek. Two other men helped Reverend Beaver, holding the candidates while he put his hands on each one's head, and as they went under the water said, "I baptize thee in the name of the Father, the Son, and the Holy Ghost." *After each baptism, there was shouting, laughing, and crying by both the person baptized and the others. There was a great deal of speaking in tongues and shouts of* "Thank you, Jesus! Praise the Lord!"

into the kingdom of God. (JOHN 3:5)

He riseth from supper, and laid aside his

Footwashing and the Lord's Supper

Footwashing is often done at the beginning of a revival, or it may be done in conjunction with the Communion service, since according to John, chapter 13, Christ washed the feet of his disciples following the Last Supper on the eve of his crucifixion. It is always considered a gesture of humility. When Eleanor Dickinson's father was a child in a small town in Kentucky, he attended a Baptist church where it was the custom for everyone to bring a towel and pail to church on Sunday morning. However, footwashing is not confined to rural Protestant churches. It has long been a custom in the Catholic Church for priests to wash one another's feet on Maundy Thursday, the anniversary of the Last Supper. Today, Pope Paul VI celebrates Maundy Thursday by washing the feet of Roman children.

REV. ROGER POWELL, *of the Church of God of the Mountain Assembly, explains his denomination's belief:* "It's written up in our bylaws to have it every quarter—you know, every three months. Now we kindly discern this. As often as you do these things, you see—as often as you do this Communion, as often as you do that, in other words—it's great. Footwashing shows humbleness and brotherly love. It's a different thing, see? You can take them both together or you can take them separate."

ELZIE PREAST, *Scrabble Creek, West Virginia:* "So the best way to do if you want to wash feet, Brother Jimmy, just get you some water, a pan, and get your shoes off—and your socks—and just wash feet. That's the best way to prove to people you believe. And while they're still stuck spinning around, talking about it, go ahead and wash feet. And enjoy yourself while they're spinning around there, stuck against footwashing. And many people are. They're against it. Well, while they're stuck, standing around and talking around there, just get away from that spirit.

"Get on up the ladder, cause it may get on you if you stick around there very long. You'll get to spinning, too, the more you spin—now this'll be a lesson for you. In the natural, I've been stuck with trucks, and seemed like the more I'd try to get out the deeper I'd bury up. Sometimes you can spin on out by spinning hard—yeah, if you find the bottom. But sometimes you don't find it. And you just keep spinning around and you just mire up deeper. And then you have to have a pull. And I've had people that I know that have had to have pulls spiritually speaking."

At one of Pappy Gube Beaver's revivals, a Communion service and footwashing were held on the same evening. First the Communion table was set up at the front of the tent. There were three chairs around

garments; and took a towel, and girded himself.

On Christ, the solid Rock I stand:
All other ground is sinking sand,
All other ground is sinking sand.

After that he poureth water into a basin,

the table. Reverend Beaver sat in one, Reverend Bledsoe, a visiting preacher, in another, and the third was left empty, reserved for Christ, the Elder Brother. Another visiting minister, **REVEREND ROBERTSON,** *served Communion and also preached to the congregation.*

"You know this will make you strong. Taking the Lord's Supper will make you strong. And if you're not right—I want you to examine yourselves tonight—if you don't take it, Brother Bledsoe won't persecute you. That's right. Brother Pappy won't persecute you if you don't take it. You know your heart, don't you? But now if you're not—if everything's not fixed up between you and the Lord—you pray and ask God to fix up everything. And he will, because he said he would. Now listen, children. This is a part of Christian life—washing feet and taking the Lord's Supper. The Lord's Supper's nothing but the bread of life. He was the bread of life. This is in remembrance of him. The Elder Brother went back. Jesus was the Elder Brother. And we are his sons and daughters, grafted in by the Lord, by his blood and his mercy. And it's a great privilege tonight, Brother Pappy, to be here.

"Washing feet will not save you tonight. No, it will not. It takes the blood of Jesus to save you. But the only thing it is, is to become humble before your brothers and sisters. And wash one another's feet. That means come humble before them. And show that you are no higher than them. The Bible says not to extend yourself more highly than your brother. Come down a little lower. May the Lord bless every one of you tonight in this, and I hope tonight, if there's anyone here sick and afflicted—if you're sick and afflicted you could get healed through this right here tonight. And if you've done something wrong and you're not right where you ought to be with God, all you have to do is raise your hand and be honest with God and say, 'God, I love you. Would you forgive me, Lord?' You know your life. You know what you've done today and how you stand with God. But I advise you, if you're not where you ought to be with God, I advise you not to take this tonight until you make things right. May God bless you."

REVEREND BEAVER: "You know this is the word of God, and we're going to bring it to you in scripture tonight. Out of the fourteenth chapter of St. Luke's Gospel. Jesus preached his disciples a sermon. This was just before he was betrayed by Judas. And he picked out the one at the table, even at the Lord's Supper, at the table he picked out the one that would betray him. God knows you better than you know yourself tonight. Amen. He knows who's betraying him tonight. He knows whether you're in condition to take this footwashing tonight, and his supper. Thank God. If you're not, as Brother Robertson said, you should get in condition.

"You'll say, 'What is the breaking of the bread?' It's his body. What is

and began to wash the disciples' feet, and to

If you want to see the Devil upset
Greet your Sister with a Holy Kiss;
    Keep your hand on the plow,
    Hold on!

wipe them with the towel wherewith he was

There is a fountain filled with blood,
Drawn from Immanuel's veins,
And sinners plunged beneath that flood
Lose all their guilty stains.

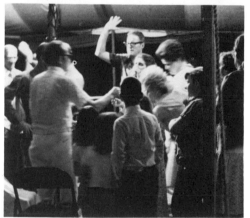

the wine? It's typical of his precious blood. If it hadn't have been for the shedding of the blood, there would have been no redemption for our sin tonight, Brother Kenneth. I'm glad of the blood, aren't you, that stained the old rugged cross? And it says here in Luke, the twenty-second chapter, 'And he took the cup . . .'—listen now—'And when he had given thanks, he took the cup and he thanked the Lord.' He thanked God. And when he had given thanks, he gave it to them and they drank all of it. He told them to drink all of it. Amen. To not just do part of it but to drink all the wine that was in the cup. And he said unto them, 'This is my blood.' Now here you are. 'This is my blood of the New Testament.' Hallelujah!—'of the New Testament, which is shed for many.' Thank God. 'And brethren, I say unto you, I will drink no more of the fruit of the vine until that day I drink it new in the kingdom of God.' Hallelujah!

"And this is very sacred tonight. This is where it should touch your heart. And I believe that when you drink this wine tonight, of his blood, that you'll be a different person. I believe that when you go down and wash your sister's or your brother's feet, you'll be a humble person in God. Hallelujah!"

It was **REVEREND ROBERTSON** *who set up the Communion table with small plastic glasses of grape juice and a platter of unleavened bread. The bread had been baked (by a woman in the community) in large wafers, later to be broken into smaller pieces and offered to the communicants.*

"Now tonight this is concerning the Lord's body and the blood of Jesus. Now this, you see me put over this chair. This represents the Elder Brother. Hallelujah! Do you feel God's power? This is for the Elder Brother, Jesus Christ. We know he's not here, but he's the head of it. It's his blood. We set this chair here for a minister. Brother Pappy, set down there. Brother Bledsoe, come here. Come on. You're a minister of the gospel. Give Brother Bledsoe a good hand." *(Clapping from the congregation.)* "Brother Bledsoe, set over here at this table. Now we break this bread, the body of Jesus. I never pass it to the congregation. If you pass it through the congregation, you're liable to embarrass someone. You got to take this willingly. You got to be able to step out and come down willingly. You got to do that. I don't want to sneak it to you or something like that. This is important. And if you don't feel like taking it, nobody's going to persecute you. Why, certainly not. You just set right where you are. But if you want to take it, you just line up down here as we break this bread. It means the body of Jesus. And this grape juice means the blood of Jesus. Jesus is the Master tonight. Now if you want to take this, you examine yourselves."

Most of the congregation came forward quietly and took Communion. When they had all returned to their seats, **REV. PAPPY BEAVER**

Master, have washed your feet; ye also ought

announced: "The more you do these things in remembrance of him, the more the Lord will bless you. Thank God, we've done partake of his body. The bread was broken and also the wine. All right, children, we're going right into the footwashing now and Brother Robertson's going to come and give you some scriptures on this."

REVEREND ROBERTSON: "Now this is found in John, the thirteenth chapter. 'He raised from the supper, laid aside his garment and took a towel and girded himself.' The Master! Jesus! Who's got all the power. 'He took the towel and girded himself.' He didn't want to be above another, did he? Jesus wanted to be humble with one another. He girded hisself and this is what happened here. Now listen very closely. 'He poured water into a basin.' Somebody get some water around here and pour it in there. Listen. 'And he began to wash the disciples' feet. And to wipe them with the towel wherewith he was girded. Then cometh he to Simon Peter; and Peter said unto him, Lord, dost thou wash my feet? Dost thou wash my feet?' Now this is what Jesus said. 'Jesus answered and said unto him, What I do thou knowest not now; but thou shalt know hereafter.' Whoooo! Hallelujah! You shall know hereafter. What about that? Amen. Jesus—Amen—was a sample for you and I. Listen to this. 'Peter said unto him, Thou shall never wash my feet.' Now listen to this. 'Jesus answered him, If I wash thee not, thou hast no part with me.' Oh glory, honey, tonight—Amen—if somebody said to pour a little axle grease on me, if it would make me a little closer to Jesus, pour it on me. Pour it on. It ain't going to hurt, anyway. Peter said, 'You're not going to wash my feet.' And Jesus, like this, he said, 'You wouldn't have no part with me.' I'll tell you what the point is. Let me tell you what the point is. I don't want to leave you on a cliff-hanger. The point is—obey the Master. Jesus answered him, 'If I wash not thou, thou hast no part with me.' Simon Peter said unto him, 'Lord, not my feet only but also my hands and my head.' And Jesus said, 'What I do, you do it one to another.'

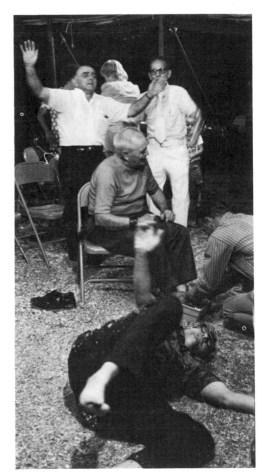

"Tonight, children, we took the Lord's Supper freely and how many felt good over it? Now this washing feet don't save you. It's an example for being humble to one another. But I tell you, if you start getting humble with one another and wash one another's feet, and love your sisters and give them a holy kiss—all right we're going to start a song and come right over here. We're going to start washing feet. God bless you, every one of you."

By the time the footwashing service in the tent had ended, a number of people were speaking in tongues, shouting, and crying. Some were rolling in the sawdust, and one man had fallen into a pan of water.

to wash one another's feet. (JOHN 13:14)

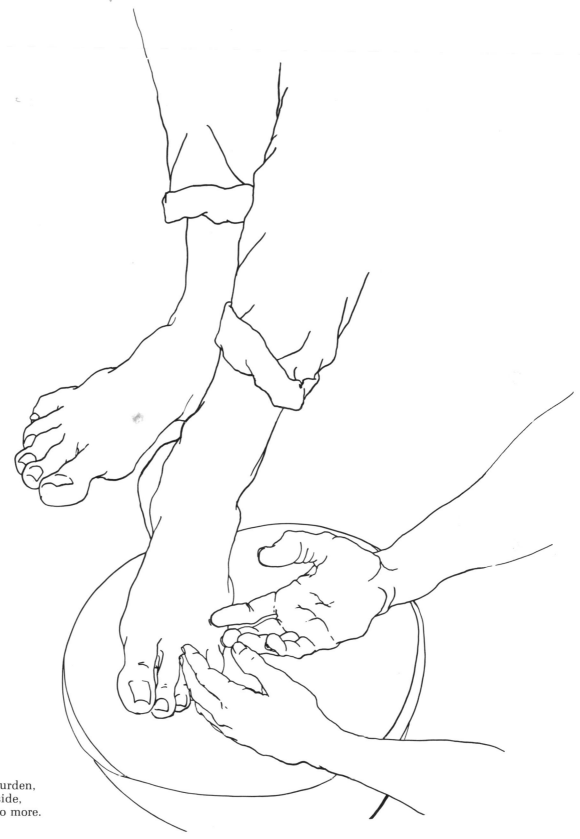

Going to lay down my burden,
Down by the river side,
I aint goin't study war no more.

Get thee behind me, Satan: thou art an offence

When, rising from the bed of death,
   O'erwhelmed with guilt and fear,
I see my Maker face to face,
   O, how shall I appear?

Satan, Whence Comest Thou?

To most of the preachers and people represented here, the devil, or Satan, is a very real personage, usually the cause of their bad habits or their misfortunes. As one Kentucky evangelist put it "The devil may be waiting at your bedside to devour you. But you are safe if you are washed in the blood of the Lamb, because the one thing that the devil cannot do is cross over the blood." The following is from a sermon heard during a Baptist revival at Valley Grove, Tennessee.

"The devil wants you to neglect your church lives, neglect your prayer lives, and nothing in the world pleases him more than for you to neglect prayer. The only way you can hold onto God is through prayer, talking to God. If you fail to do that, the devil's already got you. That's what worries me. He knows my weaknesses more than I do. You go to coasting along, the devil's already got you. If you think you've got it made, he's already got to you. The devil—sometimes he's right next to the preacher. I mean he's on the platform with the pastor! And I went to the deacons, and they said, 'Now, preacher, we've heard this all these years, but nobody's been able to prove it.' Listen to me. One day in the furnace room of that church I found a pint bottle better than half full of bootleg liquor. In the church!"

ELZIE PREAST: "Maybe you never thought of it like this, but the scripture came to me where they asked the question, 'Satan, whence comest thou?' I believe something like that. But anyway, 'Whence comest thou?' And he said, 'Going up and down through the earth, seeking whoever I may devour.' Now did you ever—now did you ever see the devil going up and down through the earth? Did he have a long chain a-dragging? Was he ugly? 'Whence comest thou, Satan?' 'From going up and down through the earth, seeking whom I may devour.'

"He may be in an automobile, and he may be in the influence of alcohol. He was in the alcohol one time when he met Brother Jimmy Withrow on the highway. Yeah, this brother right here. He was given up to die. They said he wouldn't live three hours. This brother right here—his wife and children back there. Little girl back there, little boy over here somewhere I guess. Anyway, he's got one. Anyway, Brother Jimmy met the devil on the highway, seeking. He was a-seeking. I believe that. I believe if you go down the highway tonight and you barely escape, I believe he was a-seeking you, wanting to take your life. And if you do escape, I believe Jesus is the one caused you to escape."

JIMMY WITHROW *is a young man who attends church at both Camp Creek and Scrabble Creek, West Virginia. He plays the guitar and sings duets with his wife; he also preaches and testifies—often thanking God for saving his life when he was seriously injured in an automobile. accident.*

a day when the sons of God came to present

Now God's got a Kingdom
But the Devil's got a Kingdom, too;
    Gonna tear down that Devil Kingdom
    Gonna tear down that Devil Kingdom
    Gonna tear down that Devil Kingdom
O let me tell you, brother, what I'm gonna do.

themselves before the Lord, and Satan came

"You know, people just don't understand the mercies of God. I was talking to some state police down there in Virginia. And I was telling them how far, Brother Joe, that I was threw out of that car. They told me it was over three hundred feet. One looked at the other one, and he said, 'Imagine three hundred feet. Seeing a man sail through the air.' He said, 'Do you know that's the length of a football field?'

"I said, 'Is that right? I didn't know that.' But I said, 'I'm glad I had a catcher there.' Thank God. I'm glad he was right there. You know, I thank God for every little blessing."

ELZIE PREAST *continues his sermon:* "I was going up a mountain one time with a truckload of slag, in low gear. And I seen in a vision a car coming around the curve. Before the car ever come around the curve, I seen it in a vision. And the Lord let me see it—why? So I could be on the watch. I got up a little closer to the curve and here comes the car. Around the curve. On the wrong side of the road. Over against a barrier two or three feet high where they'd rised it up around the top of the bank with dirt. And he hit that pile of dirt on the wrong side of the road—which would have been my side. And not only on the hard-top, but clear over off the hard-top. And he lost control of his car when he hit that curve, and he came around there in that shape. And I stopped right in the road. I was driving very slow. I was heavy-loaded. And when I finally stopped, Brother Turner, I'd be safe in saying that your fist wouldn't have went between the fenders of my truck and that car. Now you say the Lord doesn't show you, doesn't protect you? The Lord can warn you. He can warn you in dreams. He can let you see a vision. He can let you feel that something's coming. He said he'd show you things to come. So evidently the devil must have been seeking my life. And the Lord let me see that and he stopped him. Bless the Lord. Now whence comest thou? He may be driving an automobile, drunk. And he may be doped up. He may be smoking pot or he may be taking some kind of a shot. That's what causes people to do what they do. It's the devil."

REV. PAPPY GUBE BEAVER: "You know, if the Lord walks with us tonight, we're in good hands. We've got an insurance company come out on TV and said, if you're in their hands, you're in good hands. But I've got better news. If you're in the Lord's hands, no one can harm you. Amen. The devil may get you down, but he can't take that soul from you. Hallelujah! If you've been borned again the devil can't do nothing about it. We're going to sing another song at this time and trust this one will be a blessing to you.

JOE TURNER: "The devil can't do any more than God lets him do. Amen. I heard a man the other day—I like to hear him preach, but I thought, how ignorant the poor man sounded—Billy Graham. Now I like to hear him preach when he kindly gets right down with it. But he

79

also among them. And the Lord said unto

I think, when I read that sweet story of old,
        When Jesus was here among men,
How He called little children as lambs to his fold,
        I should like to have been with them then.

Satan, Whence comest thou?   Then Satan

O Beulah land, sweet Beulah land,
As on the highest mount I stand,
I look away across the sea,
Where mansions are prepared for me,
And view the shining glory shore,
    My heav'n, my home forevermore!

had a great audience of people there, and he made this admission. He said, I believe, 'I've been eighteen months a-making a book and trying to figure out where the devil come from.'

"Why, anybody's got their third-grade education and has sense enough to follow a stream of water would know where the devil come from. And I thought, where in the world he'd been all these eighteen months that he didn't know where the devil come from? You know this tonight? The Bible plainly said there wasn't anything made except God made it. Now that's the Bible. He was first and He was last. God created the devil, Brother Preast, whether you'll say Amens on that or not. God created the devil. And I thought as highly educated as Billy Graham is, and as many people as he's preached to, as many Bible-college people as he's come up against, looked like somebody would have told him."

and fro in the earth, and from walking up and

Free at last, free at last,
  I thank God I'm free at last.
Satan is a liar and a conjurer, too,
  I thank God I'm free at last;
If you don't mind, he'll conjure you,
  I thank God I'm free at last.

down in it. (JOB 1:6-7)   And be not drunk with

Blest be the tie that binds
Our hearts in Christian love;
The fellowship of kindred minds
Is like to that above.

Against Strong Drink

When the temperance movement got underway during the early nineteenth century, southern churches began singing antidrink songs. Evangelists in the area have never stopped preaching on the subject. Many confess to being reformed drinkers themselves, such as **REV. PAPPY GUBE BEAVER.**

"Why, people don't want the old-time religion any more. Why, it's driven out. Out of the house of God because it's too strict. They say they can't have their card games. They can't do their dances. They can't have their social drinks. They can't have their parties. They can't gather in the Congress and the courts of our land and nation without having a few beers or a few drinks of liquor or a few cocktails. I tell you the Bible speaks strongly against it. It speaks strongly against strong drinks. It will poison your mind. And many people wind up—they wind up in the institution over here at Lyons View—the Eastern State Hospital. Their brain cells are destroyed by alcohol. Come on, say Amen. It'll destroy your health. And anything that'll destroy your health and do injury to you I think is sinful. I think we ought to get rid of all these things. And the Bible says it. The world is in trouble tonight—with all the chaoses that's going on.

"I've done some awful things in my time. I've run these old hills back here, fifty years ago, drunk, half the time didn't hardly know where I's at. But Jesus forgave me of that, and he'll forgive you if you'll get down on your knees and get humble and ask him to and are willing to serve him. He'll forgive you for it. Praise the Lord. He called me from the beer joint to the pulpit.

"I recorded several years ago for Capitol Records on label as Pappy Gube Beaver. I made some records while I was in sin. But after the gospel songs come out, I got condemned hearing my own songs and got saved that way in a South Carolina jailhouse—about eighteen years ago."

Reverend Beaver would like to record more. He feels that since he has been saved and is taking care of his voice, he could do a better job. "Because I got more knowledge and more strength, and I think I sing better now than I did back when I was drinking. Somebody said the other day, said, 'Pappy, have you quit drinking?'

"I said, 'Uhn-uhn. Still drinking.'

" 'Oh,' he said, 'We didn't know that. We thought you was a-preaching.'

"I said, 'Preaching, too.'

"Said, 'What are you drinking?'

"I said, 'I'm drinking out of a different fountain than you're talking

Spirit. (EPHESIANS 5:18) Wine is a mocker,

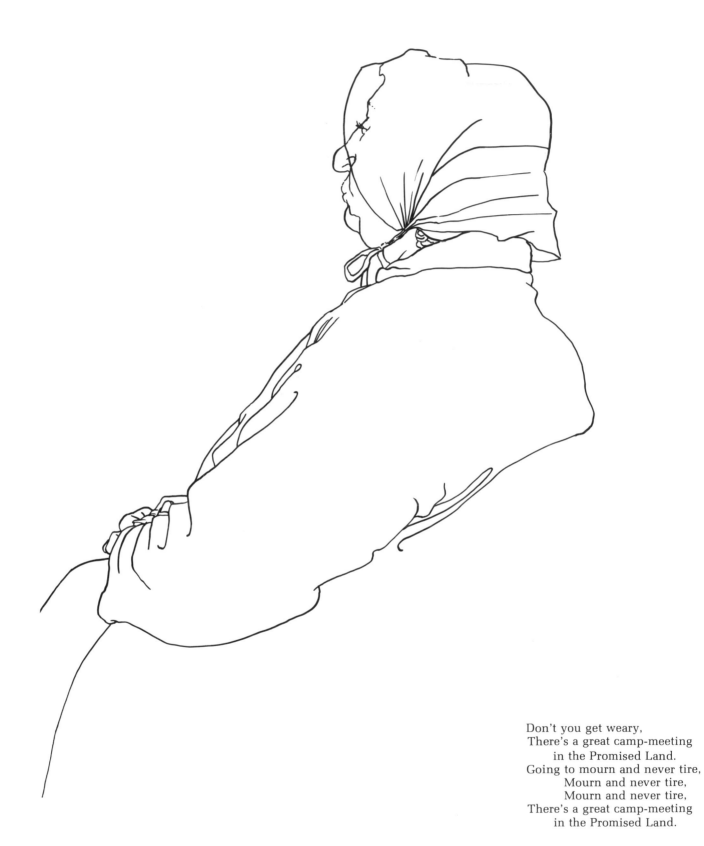

Don't you get weary,
There's a great camp-meeting
in the Promised Land.
Going to mourn and never tire,
Mourn and never tire,
Mourn and never tire,
There's a great camp-meeting
in the Promised Land.

strong drink is raging: and whosoever is deceived

about. I'm drinking out of God's fountain. God will never run dry. Hallelujah!' I said, 'I'm a-singing a song to Zion now. Used to sing to the devil.' You know, the old love songs, the old worldly songs. We used to sing them. But now I'm a-singing for Jesus. Hallelujah! I never quit singing. I'm a-singing for Jesus. Just moved over and went to drinking out of a different fountain. That fountain's coming down from God.''

ELZIE PREAST: "So if God has baptized you with the Holy Ghost, you're in the family. Just live right. Live right. Strive to live right. Not only in church or on weekends, but when you leave here. In the morning it's blue Monday they call it, you know, with a lot of people. You know what makes it blue? They get out and live like the devil on the weekend. They'll drink their booze and they'll have a good time from Friday

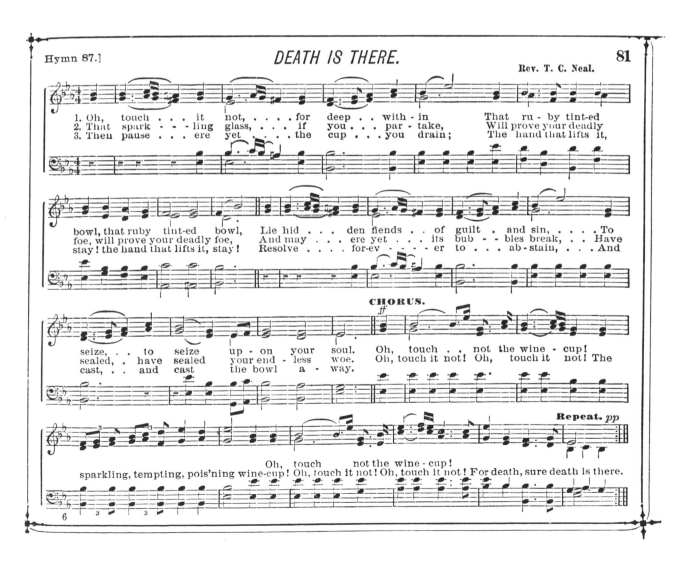

thereby is not wise. (PROVERBS 20:1)

The blood, the blood
is all my plea,
Hallelujah! it cleanseth me;

Now therefore beware, I pray thee, and drink

Alas, and did my Savior bleed, And did my Sov'reign die?
Would He devote that sacred head for such a worm as I?
Was it for crimes that I have done, he groan'd upon the tree?
Amazing pity! Grace unknown! And love beyond degree!

not wine nor strong drink, and eat not any

Nearer, my God, to Thee,
    Nearer to Thee!
E'en tho' it be a cross
    That raiseth me;
Still all my song shall be—
Nearer, my God, to Thee!
    Nearer to Thee!

evening. They'll usually start about that time, isn't it, Brother Dempsey? Bless your heart, I know. I used to drink. I know about when it started. When you get through with your week's work, then they'll start it. And they'll drink on Friday night, Saturday night, and Sunday, maybe Sunday night. And they'll wake up on blue Monday with a sour stomach. It's not only blue Monday, but it's a sour stomach. And a dizzy head. And an empty pocketbook. And maybe the wife and children all needs flour in the house. O God, what a picture! No wonder it's blue Monday for a lot of people.

"Brother, you can turn your blue Mondays into happy Mondays. You can have peace in your soul and you can have a settled stomach on Monday. I've never woke up, Brother Turner, on this new life we're talking about, with a sour stomach. Have you? Bless the Lord! I've been drunk. I've been drunk on the power of God. I fell down under the power of God—yeah, different times. I fell out under the power of God, and I never did get hurt. I never did wake up with a headache and a hangover."

REV. JOE M. MILES: "We know out on the highways it's dangerous, especially on these weekends, cause the world wants to celebrate on the weekend. They want to get a little spirits in them, get out on the highway and celebrate Friday and Saturday and Sunday night, and then they get up on Monday and the devil's jumping out of them. You can see him jumping out of their eyes. Then they'll live all week long and put up with the devil in order to be able to celebrate again. If that's all I lived for from one week to another—I told a boy the other day, I said, 'It's a crying shame, you work hard on this job and sweat and suffer all week long just to be able to drink a bottle of beer and a little liquor and have what you call a big time on the weekend.' I said, 'If that's all I got out of life, I'd just go over here and jump off the Gay Street bridge and end it all.' Amen. Thank the Lord. So let's remember these people tonight in prayer."

JASPER AND GOLD.

Hymn 1.]

THE HEAVENLY JERUSALEM.

Rev. Charles Wesley.

T. C. O'Kane.

CHORUS.

1. By faith we alread - y be - hold, The heavenly Jerusalem here;
Its walls are of JASPER and GOLD, As crystal its buildings are clear,
} The cit - y adorned with its

2. Immovably founded in grace, It stands as it ever hath stood;
And brightly its Builder displays, And flames with the glory of God.
} The city adorned

3. That cit - y so ho - ly and clean, No sorrow can breathe in the air;
No gloom of affliction or sin, No shadow of e - vil is there.
} The cit - y adorned with its

Jasp - er and Gold . . . The home of the blest, . .
with Jasper and Gold, The home of the blest, By faith we already be - hold.

would have told you. I go to prepare a place for

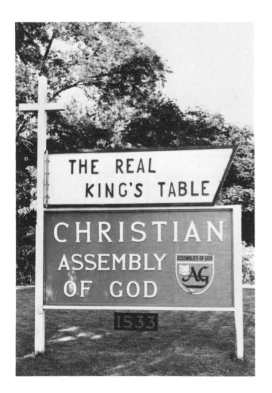

The City of Jasper and Gold

The text of the hymn on the opposite page is based on Revelation 21–22, where St. John the Divine describes his vision of the heavenly Jerusalem. Today ideas of what heaven may be like, before and after the Last Judgment, vary greatly among preachers and church members.

REV. JOE M. MILES *tells his congregation:* "Thank God! One of these days we're going to shout Thank God for ten million years. We're going to keep on shouting and keep on shouting. We're going to sit down at the table of the Lord and eat and eat and eat, Brother Ayers. And when we get through, we can go out and visit around the heavens and, thank God, the table will be ready when we come back. Isn't that going to be a wonderful place? And all the tears shall be wiped from our eyes, hallelujah! No more worries about having a job. No more worries about paying the income tax. No more worries about all those bills coming in because our God, hallelujah, will be the king of that place, and all the bills will be paid. Amen. A lot of people down here, they won't accept no responsibility. If they don't want to accept no responsibility, let them wait until they get to heaven. Amen. They want to live like they're living in heaven down here. But we're going to have to work down here, Brother Ayers. He said this is a pressing time. We've got to press our way in, sister, to the kingdom of God. Hallelujah!

"A lot of people get discouraged and downhearted and want to quit. They don't want to press. He said this is the pressing time. You read the life of the Apostle Paul. From the very day that he got saved on the road to Damascas, he didn't have nothing but trouble the rest of his life. But thank God he had this testimony that he pleased God when he came down to die. He said, 'I fought a good fight. I finished my course and I am now ready to be off.' He was hungry, beat, cast out, shipwrecked, put in prison, and everything else in the world. And through it all he held on to the unchanging hand of God. Hallelujah! How many of you feel like the Apostle Paul tonight?

"You know, our three astronauts came back from the moon today, and they were happy and rejoicing as they came back to the earth and their home. But, thank God, we're going to leave this old planet one day when we start home, and we're not going to stop on the moon or the Milky Way. Thank the Lord. We're going on into the heavens to meet with our Lord and Savior Jesus Christ. And I thought today as they were taking these astronauts to check them to see if they brought back any kind of diseases or any kind of germs back off the moon, back to this planet, back to this country of ours—they checked them closely to see what they brought back. And thank the Lord, we're not going to have to be checked when we get to heaven. Thank God, our robes are going to be washed white with the blood of our Lord Jesus Christ. And we're

you. And if I go and prepare a place for you,

Guide me, O Thou great Jehovah,
 Pilgrim thro' this barren land:
I am weak, but Thou art mighty;
 Hold me with Thy pow'rful hand:

94

I will come again, and receive you unto myself;

What a fellowship,
What a joy divine,
Leaning on the everlasting arms;
What a blessedness,
What a peace is mine,
Leaning on the everlasting arms.

that where I am, there ye may be also.

Go where the waves are breaking,
    On California's shore,
Christ's precious gospel taking,
    More rich than golden ore;

For God so loved the world, that

going to be free from disease and clean from the inside out. Hallelujah! For a million years we'll keep on shouting and praising the glory of the Lord. We're not going to have to be put in isolated places where they check us over...."

REV. PAPPY GUBE BEAVER *also discussed heaven during a sermon at his tent.* "Oh, I like that song Inez sang: 'How Great Is My God.' Thank God how great he is. Just think about it tonight. We wouldn't have been here if it hadn't been for God that freed a man that was made out of the clay of the earth and became a living soul. And then he wanted the man to have a helpmeet, and God—when he put him in the Garden of Eden—he took Adam and he performed an operation on Adam. He put him to sleep —thank God—and he took a rib out. And that's how he created woman. Out of a man's rib. There was nothing made without God. Amen. Now the scientific world we're living in today, they'll say, 'Look what science can do.' Science can do some great things. They put a man on the moon. But thank God, I don't have to have a rocket ship a-standing by to get there. When he comes, he's going to take his children up. We'll be changed in a moment—in the twinkling of an eye. The scientific world now you know has done a lot of things. But you know the Lord hung that moon up there, and they haven't done anything about it. They claim to have been up there. They've seen the moon and seen many strange things. Well, I'll tell you. The Bible said, 'Eyes would not see...' They never did get to the place called heaven. They got to the moon, but they'll never get there. God will allow us to go so far and then he'll cut us off, and that's without remedy. Can you say Amen?

"You know, you hear Christians talk about where heaven's going to be. I don't care where it is, if it's over in Beaumont or Lonsdale, just so I get there. I'm going to be satisfied. I don't worry about where it's at. All I worry about is getting there."

A MAN *in the congregation at Rev. Beaver's tent testified:* " Now if you think there's not going to always be an earth here and there'll always be people on it, you're bad wrong. Because there's going to be an earth here throughout the ages, and there's going to be people on it. There ain't no doubt about it. And the Bible says that the meek will inherit the earth. The Bible says one generation will pass away and another generation come, but this earth will abide forever. That's the Bible. The earth is going to abide. And another thing—the Bible says the meek will inherit the earth. It says it clean. I tell you, anywhere that the Lord—that Jesus said when he went away he was going to prepare a place for us and he would come and receive us—anywhere that Jesus has prepared for me, that's the place where I'll be satisfied at. Wherever it's at, no difference, just as long as he's prepared it for me, I'll be satisfied. I'll be satisfied."

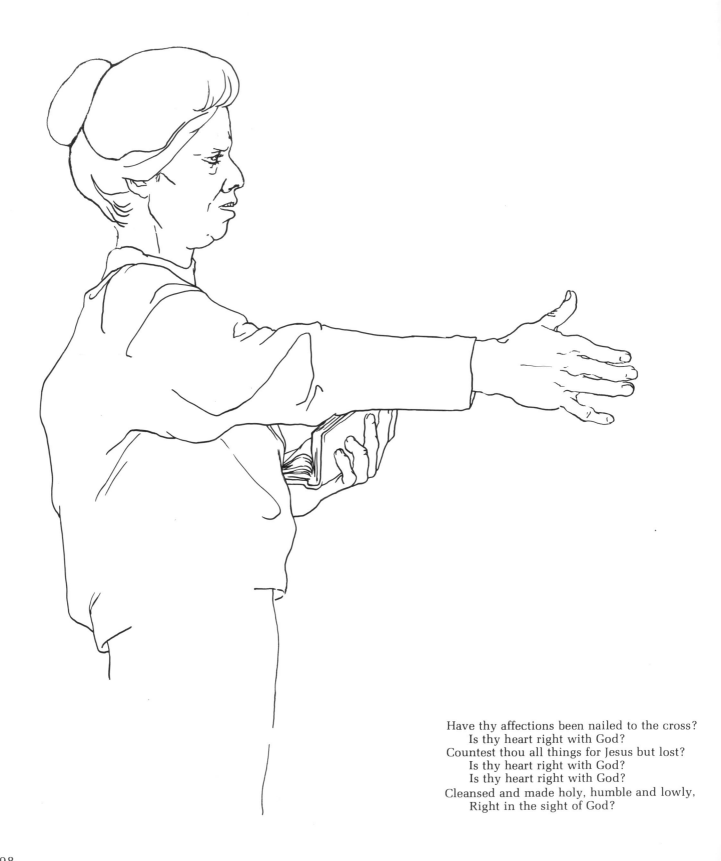

Have thy affections been nailed to the cross?
  Is thy heart right with God?
Countest thou all things for Jesus but lost?
  Is thy heart right with God?
  Is thy heart right with God?
Cleansed and made holy, humble and lowly,
  Right in the sight of God?

believeth in him should not perish, but have

Go Ye into All the World

Everyone who attends a revival is urged to spread the gospel to others. This may mean contributing to the support of foreign missions or witnessing to family and neighbors.

From a sermon heard at a revival at a small Baptist church near Sevierville, Tennessee: "I am eternally grateful to Jesus Christ for my salvation, for he purchased it upon the cross. But it took a man to tell me about it. You see, I'm not two thousand years old. I didn't live when Jesus lived here. And even though I knew how to read, I didn't read the Bible. And even though I had feet and a car and knew how to go to church and where it was, I didn't go. It took somebody who loved Jesus to come to me when I didn't want him to come and wasn't interested, but he came anyway.

"Nine out of ten of us here tonight have not only never won a soul. Nine out of ten of us in the choir tonight and in the congregation tonight have never even tried. We're like a bunch of Dead-Sea Christians. Do you know what the difference between the Dead Sea and the Sea of Galilee is? Let me tell you the similarities first of all. They're both in the Bible lands where Jesus walked and breathed and lived and died. They're also both fed by the Jordan River. The Jordan River dumps water into the Sea of Galilee, and the Jordan River dumps water into the Dead Sea, sparkling good water. The same water goes into both. And yet one is a living, thriving body of water, and you can drink from it. And the other is like its name—dead. And they say if you were able to keep a cup of water from the Dead Sea on your stomach—and you couldn't do it with the salt and other minerals and the poison in it; your body would just by nature reject it right out again—if you could contain it on your stomach, just one cup from the Dead Sea, it would kill you.

"How come they're so different? You know what happens? The Jordan River flows; it rolls right down to the Sea of Galilee, and there it is in this great big body of water. And it rolls right on out. The Sea of Galilee has an inflow and it has an outflow. It receives the water. It uses the water, and it's a beautiful body of water. But then the water goes out. It comes in and it goes out. It goes on downhill. And it comes to the Dead Sea. And it comes into the Dead Sea, and it keeps coming into the Dead Sea. And the Dead Sea doesn't give it out. There's no outflow. And the waters come in there. And they cool. And they become stagnant. And they don't grow. The fresh water evaporates and the minerals are left behind, and it's a poisonous, dead body of water. And that's the picture.

"The Sea-of-Galilee Christian is the kind that, you put the word of God in them and there's an outflow as he goes and shares it with other people. But the Dead-Sea Christian is the kind that comes to church, and he sets there and he soaks it all in and he says, 'This is great. I believe in all that's right. Keep on preaching, preacher.' But he never shares it with another. He doesn't witness to other people. He just holds it all in, and there's no outflow. And he's dead. As far as his usefulness is concerned, he's like the apple tree without the apples.''

ELZIE PREAST: "I had to teach my daddy and my mother and my brothers and some of my sisters about the Holy Ghost speaking in tongues. And I taught it to them when they didn't like it either. And I still taught it. Listen, I love my mother. And I love my brothers and sisters in the flesh. But I don't love nobody well enough to pet them without being able to tell them the truth. I don't have that kind of love. That is not love. That is deceit. That is deceit. I had to tell my mom when she was hanging her head over the bed with a sick headache and trying to vomit and gag and very sick in the body. And Dad was sitting in the living room—just the three of us there. And I got to telling them about the Holy Ghost speaking in tongues and that they ought to repent. And they was old people at that time. Dad was sitting in the living room, and I was in the bedroom, and I was telling Mom and him that. And Dad said, 'Well,' said, 'Son, this world is getting in a bad condition.'

"I said, 'Dad, Dad, I'm not talking about this world. I'm talking about you and Mom.' "

REV. CHARLES W. MATTHEWS, *First Calvary Baptist Church, Knoxville, Tennessee:* "There are over a hundred nations that have not heard about Jesus Christ. There's a lot of atheists coming out—some of them are boasting about it—that there is no God. What they done out in California, they've just about quit marrying. What they prefer is to stop marriage and take a common-law wife. Something's getting wrong with people—go to living with folks—try them out, see if they can take each other—don't like them, leave them. . . .

"And I understand—these are terrible times. The terrible things that's going on in this world. Something's wrong with this world. When men go to liking men and women go to liking women, something's wrong."

At this point there was loud laughter from the congregation.

"As Christians, we're going to have to tell the story. And the church has a responsibility. We've got to tell it, and this message has got to be put over. And a lot of people got to tell it. And we don't know how long we're going to have to try to help the world. You can't tell how long you're going to be here to help the world. I've reached the conclusion that we're going to have to hurry. I want you to go with me. I want the choir to go with me, to tell the story."

them, Go ye into all the world, and preach the

My faith looks up to Thee, Thou Lamb of Calvary:
        Savior divine;
Now hear me while I pray;
Take all my guilt away:
O, let me, from this day, be wholly Thine.

gospel to every creature. (MARK 16:15)

Great day! Great Day, the righteous marching.
Great day! God's going to build up Zion's walls,
Zion's walls
God's going to build up Zion's walls!

And they went forth, and preached every where,

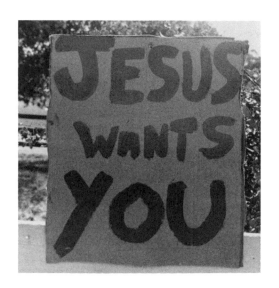

ELZIE PREAST: "If you get the spirit right, the flesh will get right. You don't have to worry about cleaning up the outside. God will clean it up from the inside. Now what got me on this was some hippies that come among us. And the way I felt about it was this: you see, there's a lot of people that thinks that nobody cares for them. And a lot of people don't care for them. As far as they're concerned, with some people, they're just out there in the world and they don't have nobody. Now there's people like that, that don't have nobody to look to to love them and to teach them and to show them the way of the Lord. And I wouldn't mistreat them. I loved them and asked them to sing with us—asked them to come up and pray with us. They bowed down and prayed. Well, some people didn't like that. And they began to holler, 'hippie this' and 'hippie that.' And throw off on people wearing long hair and long beards and one thing and another. But you see, we tried to love them and show them that we had love for them and cared for them, by letting them come in our service and not belittling them. Course they sang with us. They danced even with us. And they acted like they enjoyed themselves.

"But you see, I told these people that come among us about the Holy Ghost. I told them how to repent. The Bible said to repent and be baptized. I told them even this. I talked this thing right to their face. I said, 'Now there's people will try different things. They'll try pills. They'll smoke. They'll drink. They'll do different things, you see, trying to find satisfaction. But,' I said, 'you don't find it there. You find it only in the Lord—satisfaction.' There is no peace in the world that we're living in today. And you pretty well know it by experience, that out in the world there's toil and trouble and heartache and sorrow, this and that. And the only contentment I believe that anybody has tonight is in Jesus Christ. The Bible said, 'In the world you'll have tribulation, but in me you'll have peace.'

"Now I tried to get the church people to see like this. That you don't go to the river or the ocean catching fish to clean them before you catch them. And if there's such a thing that people is not right, and things about people that's not right, you win them first. And if you win them first, chances are that they will come on and do the things that they are supposed to do. I know I did. And I'd say that every one of us here that's got the Lord has did that. You wasn't perfect when you got the Holy Ghost. There was Brother Lucas telling tonight—and I know that that's true because I watched him outside the church. He would pull up on the outside of the church up there at Big Creek on Sunday. And it was on the night service. He would pull up outside beside the church and he would set there and puff a pipe and chew tobacco, too. Isn't that true? At the same time, I mean. And I know that he did that, see? Well now, it got to bother him. And he—he asked the Lord about it. And the

103

Lord asked him why he didn't quit. 'Why don't you quit?' Told him to quit. So I say this. If there's anything that you're doing that's not right, you first repent and try to get right with the Lord. And then all this thing that's not good will vanish. As much as you walk in the light. And that's what I was trying to get the people to see then, and I'm just as strong for it tonight as I was then. Catch the people first. Then, if they need any cleaning, you can help clean them after you catch them easier than before you catch them. I'll guarantee you.''

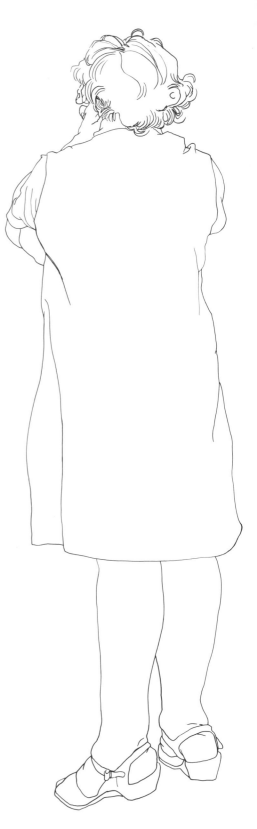

word with signs following. Amen. (MARK 16:20)

I sing because I'm happy,
I sing because I'm free—
For His eye is on the sparrow,
And I know He watches me.

...They shall lay hands on the sick, and they

Marching on, on, on to glory,
Making known the blessed story;
There is joy, joy, joy for each girl and boy,
In the Sunday-School Brigade.

And They Shall Lay Hands on the Sick

Healing through faith is an important part of a revival. The preacher and often several members of the congregation usually put their hands on the sick person's head while praying for his recovery. This is so that the Holy Ghost may enter his body. The sick person may raise his hands, cry out, tremble, or fall backwards. If he does, there will probably be someone there to catch him. **REV. PAPPY GUBE BEAVER** *practices healing in this way at almost every service.*

"Here's a little woman that's come for prayer. Those who want to stay and pray with her raise your hands tonight. Heavenly Father!

"The Bible says if there are any sick among you, let them call for the believers and elders in the church and lay hands on them and they shall recover [James 5:14-15.] And God, we don't want no honor and glory. But we pray, Lord that you'll touch this woman. The hurting is in her shoulder, Lord. Give her relief, Lord. It shall be moved. And we believe in you for it, God. I can feel the healing virtue of Jesus going through her body even now. And in Jesus' precious name we pray and ask you, God, this prayer to be granted, and we'll give you glory. Hallelujah! Praise God! The hurting is already gone. I believe it's gone. Hey, she says she didn't feel the pain now. It's gone! See what God can do for you!

"Hallelujah! Hallelujah! Thank you, Jesus. Thank you, Lord. I believe I waited a little late to have this prayer for the sick. Thank God. Hallelujah! Anybody else wants prayer? We'll stay around and pray for you.

"I know there's strength in the Lord. I know that God could teach you tonight. He's touched me so many times. He gave me my voice here the other night. I took the thing from the drugstore, and instead of helping me it made me worser. I hate to say this, but my throat got worser.

"When I got down on bended knee and began to cry out to God, last night, Grandma White, my voice got clearer. Why, you couldn't tell I'd ever been hoarse. And one of the men in the congregation said, 'Haven't none of you noticed the miracle tonight?' And nobody said nothing, and he said, 'Brother Beaver! God touched his voice and it's opened up clear.' Hallelujah!"

One evening when Rev. Pappy Beaver gave his altar call, a woman got out of a car and walked a few steps toward the tent. **MEMBERS OF THE CONGREGATION** *rushed to meet her and helped her the rest of the way, shouting,*

"It's the will of God!"
"Glory hallelujah!"
"Who said God isn't real?"

you? let him call for the elders of the church;

"Who said she couldn't?"
"God is moving, children. Amen!"
"That woman come walking in here."
"Thank God!"

ONE MAN WEARING OVERALLS *stood up and shouted, "God told me she could!" The woman, unable to walk or help herself in any way, had been left by her family in the care of a hired nurse-companion. The nurse had driven her patient to the revival and parked her car as close to the tent as possible. After the sick woman had walked into the tent, the man in overalls testified further.*

"You know, I was talking here at the first of the service. I told you I could tell you something. Honey, I knew that woman would get out of that car. I knowed that woman could walk. I knowed that lady knowed what was going on. My wife went out there and talked to her. The lady said she had the mind of a child, didn't she? Yes, she did. My wife went over and talked to her, said, 'Honey, how are you feeling?'

"Said, 'Just fine,' but said, 'I'm a-hurting from right here to here.' But she had the mind of a child? I don't believe she's got the mind of a child. I sure don't. Praise God. You know, I think God done it!" (*Shouts of Amen.*)

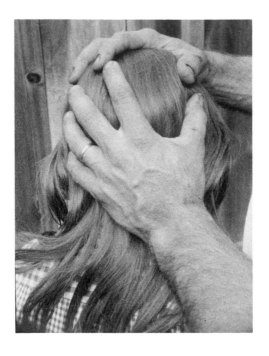

"I've seen so many things happen. I'm one of those fellows that believes anything I see. Now Brother Hailey, he preaches divine healing. Brother Hailey, he was eat up with TB. As the old folks used to say, 'old consumption.' He went to an island. He went there to die or for God to heal him. He went out on the sand, and the buzzards had done flocked around him. And he was praying, and he turned his head. And he spit upon the sand. And he spit up that rotten stuff. God healed him. He had on a pair of white shoes, and he wore them all the time. I told my wife, I said, 'I want a pair of white shoes like Brother Hailey's.' Honey, I've got them. I've had them for two years. Clean them up, they look like they're brand new. I've shouted in them. People have shouted all over them and done everything else. They're my holy shoes."

REV. ROGER POWELL *has a reputation for healing in the community of Lake City, Tennessee:* "Now I don't know whether I've ever told you this or not. It might be interesting to you. I've been fortunate for twenty-four years not to have any medication—any kind of curing—in my life. Just prayer and faith is all I've ever reached for. And I've had some serious—heart attack three years ago and various other things has happened to me—colds, flu, coughs, pneumonia fever, and everything else has been wrong with me. But it's all been healed through prayer. Not with the aid of one taste of anything. Period. And I've been able to

and let them pray over him, anointing him

High o'er the hills the mountains rise,
Their summits tow'r toward the skies;
But far above them I must dwell,
Or sink beneath the flames of hell.

with oil in the name of the Lord. (JAMES 5:14)

A sunbeam, a sunbeam,
    Jesus wants me for a sunbeam,
A sunbeam, a sunbeam,
    I'll be a sunbeam for Him.

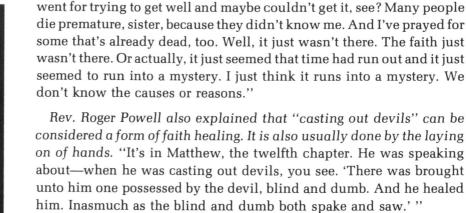

do that for twenty-four years. And if the country would have been that fortunate, they would have been blessed with billions of dollars that's went for trying to get well and maybe couldn't get it, see? Many people die premature, sister, because they didn't know me. And I've prayed for some that's already dead, too. Well, it just wasn't there. The faith just wasn't there. Or actually, it just seemed that time had run out and it just seemed to run into a mystery. I just think it runs into a mystery. We don't know the causes or reasons."

Rev. Roger Powell also explained that "casting out devils" can be considered a form of faith healing. It is also usually done by the laying on of hands. "It's in Matthew, the twelfth chapter. He was speaking about—when he was casting out devils, you see. 'There was brought unto him one possessed by the devil, blind and dumb. And he healed him. Inasmuch as the blind and dumb both spake and saw.' "

Another Pentecostal preacher states that a devil is a "spirit inside you which could cause you to do mean things, like someone wanting to steal things all the time or lust after a woman." Most agree that a person can be possessed of more than one devil at once, and if faith is strong enough these devils can be cast out.

According to the Book of Acts 19:11-12, "And God wrought special miracles by the hands of Paul: so that from his body were brought unto the sick handkerchiefs or aprons, and the diseases departed from them, and the evil spirits went out of them." If someone is too ill to come to a revival, the preacher may send the sick person a prayer cloth. These cloths are also distributed in hospitals. A prayer cloth may be a handkerchief or any piece of cloth anointed with oil—olive oil from the Holy Land if it is obtainable. Anyone can bring a handkerchief to a revival to have it anointed and prayed over by the evangelist. It can be then reserved for future illnesses. Anointing with oil is also sometimes used along with the laying on of hands, although some preachers think it is unnecessary.

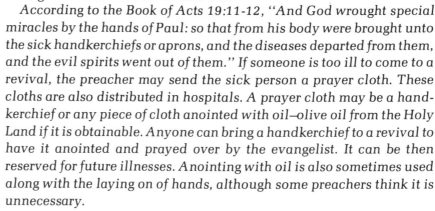

The following quotation is from a testimony by **A WOMAN** *at a Holiness revival near Clinton, Tennessee:* "I've had trouble with my hip for about twelve years, and I had been in constant pain with it. Not pain, but—you know—aggravation. And the Lord healed that. And I haven't had any more trouble with that. And well, one night I went home and—I guess it's because I wear my boots so much—I'd gotten athlete's foot. And I was wanting something to put on it. I went to the medicine cabinet. I didn't have anything in the first place cause we threw all that out years ago. And I took one of Brother Leonard's prayer cloths, and I put it on my toe. And I got up the next morning and that raw meat was healed. It was well."

AN ELDERLY MAN *at the same revival:* "Well, He opened up my lungs. The other night I was all chugged up. Couldn't get a good breath." *The man further testified that now he could "breathe good" and without pain. His wife got up to explain that he had emphysema and had been having trouble sleeping because he couldn't get his breath, but that now he was "sleeping like a baby." She also testified that God had healed her of a heart condition several years before.*

One evening A YOUNG WOMAN *walked several miles to a revival in Sunset Gap, Tennessee, to dedicate her life to God so that her sick child might live. During most of the service she stood on tiptoe, her arms outstretched, trembling, crying, and speaking in tongues. She insisted that her baby would be well by the time she reached home, "because I've given my life to Christ in exchange for his."*

REV. JOE M. MILES: "Sister Douglas, she's still not healed by a long shot, still may have to go to the hospital. Let's remember her. Carlene's going to be going to the hospital tomorrow, and let's remember her in prayer tonight. God reaches down and touches people. My God is able, isn't he? Amen. I tell you, if we don't start believing in God a little bit, the Pentecostal people is going to have to build them a hospital. The Catholics got them one, the Baptists got them one, the Presbyterians got them a hospital. And this leaves the Pentecostals and Methodists out. So we just might as well, if we don't get some faith and get ahold of the hand of God, we just might as well build us a hospital. Call it the Pentecostal Faith Hospital. *(Laughter from the congregation.)*

"Cause we got no faith. So the Pentecostal Faith will have to build them a hospital. Now we don't have to have a hospital if we believe in God. Amen.

"We preach our faith but don't practice it. Have faith is a verb, and that denotes action, ready to move out and help the helpless tonight. I know my God is able. Hallelujah! He's able to touch and heal every one of these tonight if they'll only believe God. You know God has performed miracles in the past. God healed me of heart trouble when five doctors gave me up and said there was nothing they could do. But my God came to see me with the touch that healed.

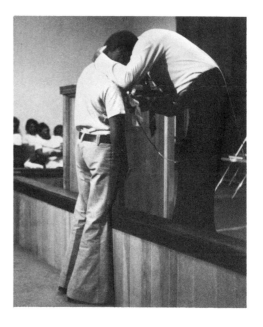

"Trouble about us is, we just run to the medicine cabinet sometimes and get us some BC and aspirins or Stanback. Fellow told me the other day, said, 'Why do you want to bother God for a little old headache? Well, I could always get an aspirin or a Stanback, take it, and I wouldn't have to bother the Lord. But you don't bother God. God wants us to come to him in prayer with our troubles and our sorrows and our heartaches and our pains and our sufferings. That's just what he wants us to do, to learn to trust God. Now if we can learn to trust God with the little things, it'll be easier to trust God for the big things. Amen."

the sick handkerchiefs or aprons, and the

O Lord, send the pow'r just now,
   Lord, send the pow'r just now;
   Lord, send the pow'r just now,
And baptize ev'ry one.

diseases departed from them, and the evil

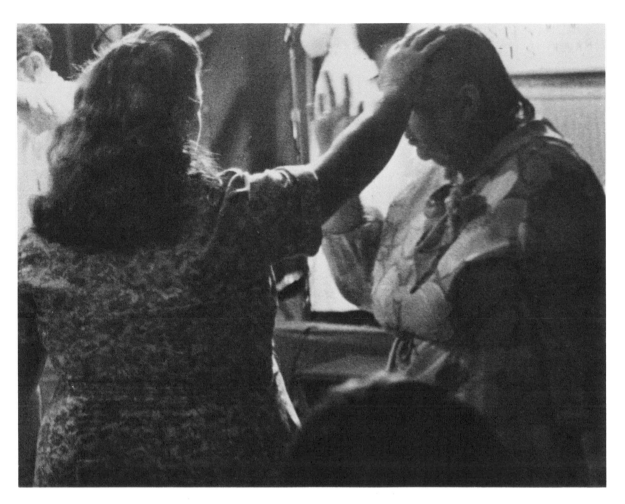

spirits went out of them. (ACTS 19:11-12)

Oh, heal it by thy grace,
Oh, heal it by thy grace;
For thou canst heal the deepest wound,
Oh heal it by thy grace.

And the prayer of faith shall save the sick...

Prayer for the Sick and Others

When a visiting evangelist held a revival at the Scott Street Assembly of God in Knoxville, Tennessee, JOE M. MILES *as regular pastor was officially on vacation. It was true that he did not have to prepare sermons. However, his days were spent in visiting the sick or others in need, and every evening he was at the church leading his congregation in prayer. The following are excerpts from his prayer requests during the ten days of the revival.*

"Glory, glory, hallelujah! Hallelujah! Thank the Lord. That's one thing we can do tonight is take our burdens to the Lord. And the Lord is able to hear and answer our prayer. He is able to help us and fight our battles. We just never learn, Sister Carter, to put our trust in God. Amen. God is able tonight. We're going to go to the Lord in prayer. My wife was telling me about a boy, sixteen-year-old boy, that's had arthritis ever since he's about two or three months old, wasn't it, honey? Very young. And his mother said she just had to help him get up and down the steps. At one o'clock or four o'clock in the morning he would take a couple of aspirins then so he'd be able to get out of bed the next day and be able to walk. I know my God is able to touch that boy's body and heal him and make him whole. So tonight I'd like us to pray and remember that boy in this prayer. Also Sister Ledgerwood wants a very special prayer for her tonight. She's not feeling too good in body. Just came back from her home a while ago, praying for her. She can't hardly get her breath. Let's remember her tonight in this prayer. Sister Carter wants us to remember her in prayer. She's trying to get her boy in the hospital at Johnson City—the veterans' hospital—in the morning. And we're going to leave early in the morning and take him to the hospital to see if we can get him in. So let's remember to pray about that. He certainly needs for God to touch his body. Brother Bean's still in the hospital in bad condition, him and Brother Charley Hinton both. Let's remember them in prayer tonight. All right, any more requests for prayer? Glad to have Sister Lowe here with us tonight, looking a whole lot better. We appreciate her coming out to the house of the Lord. She had a serious operation, but I told her a while ago, I said, 'This mercy of the Lord certainly helped you.' She loves the Lord, God bless her. Amen. All right, any more requests for prayer? Every night this week we're doing this in this revival. Any more requests? Let's all stand and raise your hands and go to the Lord in a word of prayer. Each one of us pray from the heart."

Reverend Miles begins his prayer in tongues. There is shouting from the congregation and music in the background.

"All right, I believe at this time we'll go to the Lord in prayer. A girl called me today and her husband's having some trouble. She said, 'Brother Miles, he stays out sometimes all night long. Doesn't come in till in the morning hours.' And said, 'You know, you've been awful good to me and my husband and baby.' And said, 'We got the utmost confidence in the world in you,' and said, 'I'd like for you to come over here in the morning—early in the morning so you could catch him at home.' Said, 'I don't think he'll be here tonight.' She said, 'I'd like for you to come over and talk to him.' And this girl—I'm not going to describe her condition cause if I did, some of you'd know who she was. She didn't want me to tell. But this girl physically is in very bad condition. Fact about it, she's practically a bed patient. And she needs help. They have this child. And her husband needs help. And in the morning, if it's God's will, early in the morning I'm going to go over to their home and visit with them. And she said, 'Don't tell him that I called and asked you to come.' And I'm going to their home in the morning, as early as I can get over there, and pray with them. I'd like you to be praying, too, when I go to this house and pray for this boy. She said she might have to go back to the hospital for a time or two. Her nerves were all upset, staying there all night waiting, not knowing what time, or how, he's coming in. And it certainly is a pitiful case, and if anybody in the world needs prayer, this young girl and her husband needs prayer tonight. So let's remember them in this prayer. All right, any more requests for prayer?''

A WOMAN *in the congregation stands to speak:* "Let's remember Nadine in prayer. I reread her letter today to answer it. She talks of what she's having to go through now. One of her prayers was answered, and her family's back together, but she—she's away from Knoxville and she can't find a church to go to in Ohio. She's really having it hard. She really needs our prayers.''

REVEREND MILES: "Thank you, Sister Jennings. I was just worrying about Nadine. And I thought of the way she was always singing and helping in the church. And some of them talked like she might be able to come back, but I guess she's going to stay there. And you know—a lot of you know—and I guess she wouldn't care for me telling you. But her daddy's a backslider. And he's been a preacher—a Baptist preacher and he backslid on the Lord. And I know it hurts Nadine because she's been filled with the Spirit now, and she knows more about what it means to live for God, knows more about her daddy. Let's pray for him. God, get ahold of that man's heart. God, take hold of his heart and bring him right back here to Tennessee. Give him a church round here somewhere so he can pastor it, you know it, in this city. God can do that tonight, if we believe God. And let's pray that Nadine, in her home up there, she'll find a place there and be going to worship God.

"There's a man told me a while back that he went into a church in

removed, and be thou cast into the sea; and

My Lord calls me,
He calls me by the thunder;
The trumpet sounds within my soul,
I've not got long to stay here.
    Steal away, steal away,
    Steal away to Jesus.
    Steal away, steal away home,
I've not got long to stay here.

shall not doubt in his heart, but shall believe

I'm goin' to sit down at the welcome table,
I'm goin' to sit down at the welcome table,
Some of these days, Hallelujah

those things which he saith shall come to pass;

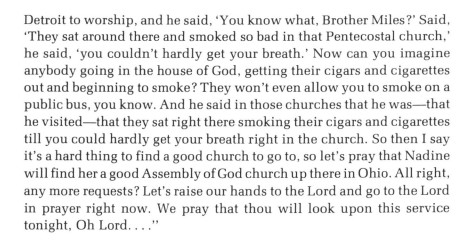

Detroit to worship, and he said, 'You know what, Brother Miles?' Said, 'They sat around there and smoked so bad in that Pentecostal church,' he said, 'you couldn't hardly get your breath.' Now can you imagine anybody going in the house of God, getting their cigars and cigarettes out and beginning to smoke? They won't even allow you to smoke on a public bus, you know. And he said in those churches that he was—that he visited—that they sat right there smoking their cigars and cigarettes till you could hardly get your breath right in the church. So then I say it's a hard thing to find a good church to go to, so let's pray that Nadine will find her a good Assembly of God church up there in Ohio. All right, any more requests? Let's raise our hands to the Lord and go to the Lord in prayer right now. We pray that thou will look upon this service tonight, Oh Lord. . . .''

"We're going to go to the Lord in prayer at this time. Elsie's girl Carlene was operated on this afternoon, so let's remember her in prayer. She's getting along good. The doctor said there wasn't any roots on this place that they removed, and said they didn't think it was cancer, so they're happy and proud about that. So let's remember her tonight in this prayer. And Brother Bean, he said he wanted everybody to remember and pray for him, and he's feeling better—in the hospital. He had this heart attack but he's getting along good. All right, any more requests for prayer? This young boy, what's his name, this young boy?''

A woman's voice replies from the congregation.

"That's right. Lee Russell. He's in Vietnam. Has fifteen more days to stay in Vietnam till he gets to come home, and he's just a nervous wreck, Sister Carter said. And he's afraid he's going to be killed before he gets his time up. Now let's remember him tonight in prayer, not only him, but let's remember the other boys. Let's remember these fellows that are negotiating for peace. Let's pray for the leaders and officials of our country. I tell you they're a lot of boys praying in Vietnam. And a lot of people in America need to be in Vietnam to wake them up a little bit, get them started praying. A lot of Pentecostal people, they need a few lead bullets sailing over their heads and bombs dropping about to get them stirred up. You know we're rested inside today. We've got good jobs, good clothes, good automobiles, nice homes to live in, and we're just unconcerned. We're sleeping. We need to stir. A lot of people are worried today about the finance in America today, the stability of our money. And all of our gold's about gone. It may take a depression to stir this country, to wake this country up and get them back to God. If that's what it takes, God says he's going to do it. I noticed the President today talking about the war in Vietnam, and he said, 'We've made all the

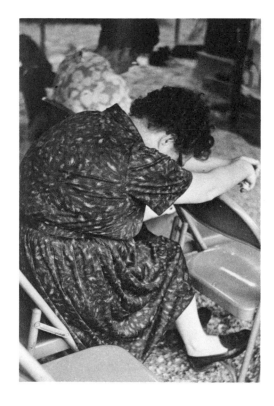

he shall have whatsoever he saith. Therefore

The hill of Zion yields a thousand sacred sweets,
Before we reach the heavenly fields, or walk the golden streets.

I say unto you, What things soever ye desire,

"Almost persuaded" Now to believe;
"Almost persuaded" Christ to receive;

when ye pray, believe that ye receive them,

Will there be any stars, any stars in my crown
    When at evening the sun goeth down?
When I wake with the blest,
In the mansions of the rest,
Will there be any stars in my crown?

and ye shall have them. (MARK 11:23-24)

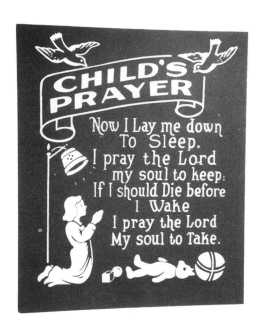

concessions that we're going to make. We're going way out beyond any reason to try and bring this war to a close.' Well now, let's pray. When man has done all he can do there, that's when God is ready to come in. All right, any more requests for prayer? If there are no more requests, let's everyone stand. Raise your hands toward heaven. Listen as we pour out our hearts to God, will you?"

"Thank you, Sister Babcock. The singing there was good. Amen. And now let's get on over to Brother Charley Hinton. Let's remember him in prayer because he certainly needs our prayers. His wife's here with us tonight, and Brother Charley is having a very hard time after his operation. Told me today that he's still running a high temperature. Said he tried to get up and walk a little bit and said one of his legs just kind of wobbled. And his neck's kind of stiff. You know, they had to go into the back of his neck to operate on his spine.

"And then there was this young man in the intensive care unit there. I didn't talk to him because I couldn't talk to him. He was in an automobile wreck. A trailer ran into him here about five weeks ago. A twenty-five-year-old boy. Been in bed now for five weeks. Got out of the army OK, got out on the highway, and a trailer truck run into him and he's unconscious. Never spoken a word the last five or six weeks. Lays there in that bed with one hand stretched up, his face all swollen. Looks like he's about fifty years old. He's only twenty-five years old, his mother said. And let's remember him tonight. He's never spoken a word. The doctor's not giving him any hope to speak. Just laying there, just a bunch of flesh there breathing, that's about all. I looked at him there this afternoon, and I thought, now if Jesus was passing by this room, he could just lay a hand on or speak the word and that boy would come back to his self, normal, walk out of the hospital. So today let us believe God. Is God alive? Is he able to walk up and down the hospital aisles? Amen. Is he about to touch this boy's body as when he walked the sandy shores of Galilee? He's the same yesterday, today, and forever-more. So let's believe God tonight for that young man in that awful condition there, and pray for his mother, too. He's not married, but let's pray for his mother.

"We pray thee, Father Lord, that thou will bless the sick and afflicted tonight. We pray, O God, that thou will touch Brother Charley tonight. He's running a high fever. Give him peace. Give him, O God, rest tonight. Let him sleep and rest good tonight. Remove all the pain and the suffering from his body tonight. Make him whole. We need the Holy Ghost moving among us here tonight, the power and glory of the Lord Jesus Christ. And now, in Jesus name we pray for everyone. . . ."

Music begins in the background and gradually obscures the prayer.

And these signs shall follow them that believe;

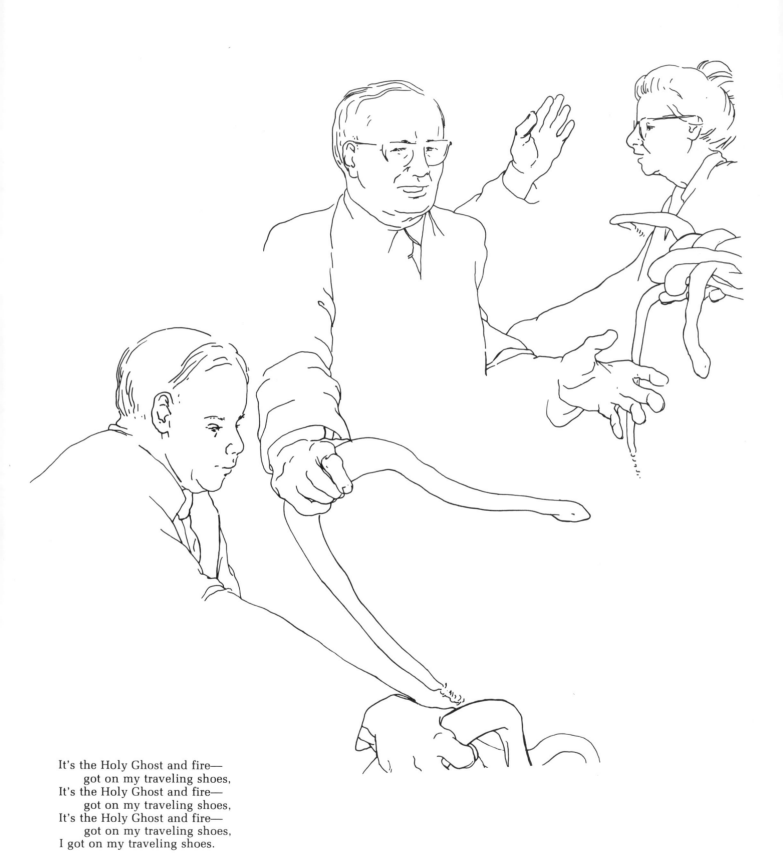

It's the Holy Ghost and fire—
    got on my traveling shoes,
It's the Holy Ghost and fire—
    got on my traveling shoes,
It's the Holy Ghost and fire—
    got on my traveling shoes,
I got on my traveling shoes.

In my name shall they cast out devils; they

They Shall Take up Serpents

Elzie Preast and Joe Turner preach and testify at one another's services, and many members attend both churches. This means they may go to church three or four nights a week, with services lasting from four to six hours. There are many such small churches in rural West Virginia. They are generally called Holiness, but many are unaffiliated. Though they share many beliefs with other Pentecostal sects, these churches place particular emphasis on the Gospel according to St. Mark, chapter 16: "And these signs shall follow them that believe; In my name shall they cast out devils; they shall speak with new tongues; They shall take up serpents; and if they drink any deadly thing, it shall not hurt them; they shall lay hands on the sick and they shall recover." Thus they are chiefly known for their practices of handling poisonous snakes in church and drinking strychnine to demonstrate their faith.

The snakes, usually rattlesnakes or copperheads native to the mountains of West Virginia, are caught in the spring, often by people in the community who sell them to the churches. They are released in the fall so that they can hibernate and breed in their natural habitat. During the summer they are kept in the homes of church members and brought to church in boxes. A serpent box is about three feet long, with a screen at one end and a padlocked lid. At some time during the service, usually while music and dancing is also going on, a preacher will unlock the box, reach in and pick up one or more snakes. Anyone in the congregation may come forward and reach for a snake if he or she feels moved to do so. However, Eleanor Dickinson never saw anyone persuaded or urged to pick up a snake. She did see many people voluntarily hold them for a few minutes or for as long as a half-hour, then return them to the preacher. Although the singing, dancing, and shouting may become loud and frenzied, the handling of snakes is done calmly, with care to keep them out of the reach of small children. A person who has successfully handled and "won a victory over the serpent," may cry out, "Hallelujah!" or "Thank you, Jesus!" When a visitor in the congregation at Scrabble Creek rose and asked why it was necessary to handle snakes during the service, ELZIE PREAST explained his belief.

"I don't handle them every time. I really don't feel like it's necessary every time for me. But it does say, 'They shall take up serpents.' And Jesus is the one's doing the talking. Said, 'They shall take them up.' Well, I've got to do it, or somebody's got to do it, or else it makes Jesus out a liar, because if I tell you you *shall* go out that door, it means that you've got to go out there, one way or the other. Now listen how it reads. 'And these signs shall follow them that believe.' *Shall.* Now if it said, 'If you feel led to handle them, if you believe to handle them,' it'd be kind of different. But it says, 'These signs *shall* follow.' See, it's just like the

Holy Ghost speaking in tongues. It don't come any other way. And when I read it says they shall speak with new tongues, they've got to do like it says. But the scriptures said that they shall pick up serpents, and somebody has to do that. If we don't do it, Jesus can raise up a people that will do it. If it's the least baby here tonight. If it's this little baby, if we won't do it, he'll raise them little children up here in our midst. Or maybe somebody that's never been born. But he's going to have somebody that will do it. If we don't do it, he'll have somebody that will do it.

"But we can have service without serpents being in it. I'm just as happy sometimes without them as I am with them. I went to church over at Brother Turner's the other Sunday night. He'd a had them there that night. But he told me he was rushed to get started over there. And you know he keeps them in boxes, and when they're not too clean, why, he don't like to bring them to church. He likes to kind of bath them up a little bit. I think any time that you would get in a form so much that you had to have anything—if we didn't have any music here tonight, we could still pray. And we could still testify and read the Bible. But music is a part of it, too. It says, 'Praise him on stringed instruments.' "

A revival at Scrabble Creek or Camp Creek is always well attended —often by people from neighboring states where snake handling is illegal. Sometimes chartered buses bring whole congregations to West Virginia from as far away as Florida. **ONE MAN** *who had come from North Carolina told Joe Turner's congregation at Camp Creek:*

"We ought to give Brother Turner more money. He said he was behind in his bills. You know, to me it's a great privilege to come to a place like this where you can say about what you want to and do about like you want and do as you feel in the way of the Lord. Now where I come from it's against the law to handle serpents. The last man that got caught doing it, he served thirty days on the road and paid a fine for it. Now, good folks, you just don't know how thankful you ought to be. And I believe with a place like this—you know we had one free place down there at Durham. It was the Burning Bush in Durham. And the people just kept slacking off and wouldn't come. And those that would come wouldn't give. So the Burning Bush is closed up today. Now it's just as much a part of living right. It's all right to get up here and dance. It's all right to handle you a snake. It's all right to preach or do anything else you want to. But unless God has control of your pocketbook, you're not a bit of good."

ANOTHER YOUNG MAN *who had traveled from California to worship at Camp Creek came forward and testified:* "I just want to say, I came here nine months ago, and I took pictures for a magazine on the West Coast. That's how I got here. And that's how I met Elzie. I remember him

up serpents; and if they drink any deadly

Abide with me:
Fast falls the eventide;
The darkness deepens; Lord, with me abide:
When other helpers fail, and comforts flee,
Help of the helpless, O, abide with me!

thing, it shall not hurt them; they shall lay

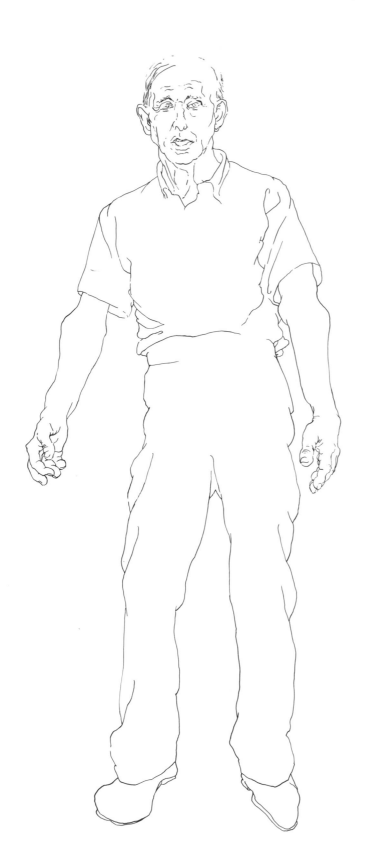

There's a great day coming, A great day coming,
There's a great day coming by and by;
When the saints and the sinners
    shall be parted right and left,
Are you ready for that day to come?
Are you ready for the Judgement Day?

hands on the sick, and they shall recover.

talking about when he was eighteen—that you went to church, and you were on alcohol. And you sat in the back and realized that they had something that you lacked. And I was sitting back there hearing you say that and feeling the same thing. I was just sitting back there—even though I was getting paid a lot of money from this magazine to come here and take pictures—I knew that you all had something that I didn't have. And I realized that I wanted to have that, too. I wanted to be with the Spirit of God. Well, I went back to California. I got baptized there. But they don't have the Spirit there like they do here. Well, I've seen the power. I've seen the power and the work of Jesus and it's moved me to change my life. And I just wanted to thank you for my life, and to thank God that I'm alive and I can be here again."

ELZIE PREAST: "The Lord bless you. We're glad you're here. And I hope the Lord will bless you wherever you go. We're happy to have you here. You never know what you might do for other people. But I believe the Lord has something in sending people here so that they can take it to bless other people we wouldn't be able to reach. His word will be spread. You know, since maybe five or six years ago—could be even longer than that. Time goes so fast—whenever they started coming here. And then they tried to pass a law. It was introduced in the legislature to outlaw serpent handling in the state of West Virginia in church services, like you see here tonight. And it was defeated by one of the senators named Bob Holliday. I don't know whether you've ever heard his name mentioned, but Bob Holliday stands for freedom of worship. Yeah, I guess it's the only state where it's not illegal to handle serpents.

"We've had a lot of publicity and we really didn't ask for it. One fellow got up here one night, right along up in here somewhere a few years ago, and he said, 'I see you all have made headlines.'

"I said, 'Yeah, we didn't ask for that.'

"And he said, 'Well, Preacher so-and-so down at Charleston's been trying to get them to advertise his services, and they said they wouldn't do it.'

"Now you think you can keep God's people down? No. No. Uhn-uhn. God's people's not going to be kept down. God's going to raise them up. It makes no difference who don't like them. Bless the Lord."

It is true that snake handling has been outlawed in most states, since a certain number of people have died as a result of the practice. Countless others, however, have been bitten and survive. They usually refuse medical aid. When Eleanor Dickinson first met Joe Turner his left hand was swollen and discolored. When she drew his portrait he was holding two rattlesnakes with his right hand, since his left was still useless.

So then after the Lord had spoken unto them,

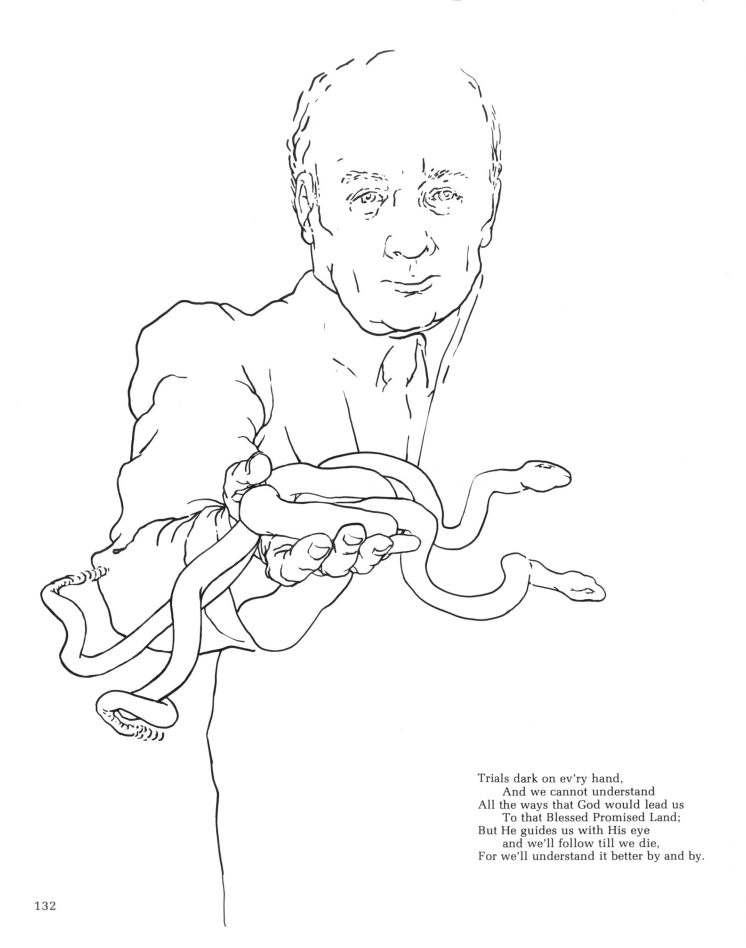

Trials dark on ev'ry hand,
    And we cannot understand
All the ways that God would lead us
    To that Blessed Promised Land;
But He guides us with His eye
    and we'll follow till we die,
For we'll understand it better by and by.

ELZIE PREAST: "Brother Turner recovered here the other Sunday night from a snakebite. It's been five weeks tomorrow night. Hold up your hand. Is there anybody here that's never seen anyone bit with a rattle-snake like that? This man, I guess if they'd a left it up to some of them, he'd have been pronounced dead. Cause I think they said that he done died, when they come into church. They's wringing their hands and crying. As far as he's concerned, I guess he was gone. He didn't know anything about what was going on, and he was speechless. Looked like he couldn't say anything hardly that you could understand. Well, you can still read it in the Bible. 'They shall lay hands on the sick. . . .' Now my wife sent for me to come out there, where they's at in front of the church. And there was some scared almost in as bad shape as probably Brother Turner. And some of them I'd say was worse cause they didn't have Jesus in their life. Was in worse shape. If Brother Turner had died, I had hopes that he'd go on to a better place, wherever it's at. But there's some there that didn't have the Lord. And they was in a lot worse shape than he was. They was in trouble over him, crying and wringing their hands.

"I stayed in here and tried to entertain the people that was in a lot of trouble mixing around. Until I was sent for. And whenever they sent for me, I went out there, and I laid my guitar about halfway to the church alongside of something as I went. And I put my hands on Brother Turner's face, and I said, 'Jesus, rebuke this death spirit off Brother Turner.' "

JOE TURNER: "Seemed like about in minutes I was paralyzed. Couldn't help myself. And my tongue started to get numb. And my throat started getting numb. And it just seemed like the whole world was a glitter of fire that I was setting myself. You see, I couldn't—couldn't control myself. And seemed like—I don't know whether it bothers you or not, but if I lay my head under a cover, like I'd sleep with it, it smothers me. I can't get my breath right. Well now that bothers you a lot when you're serpent-bit. Seemed like I was getting my breath but it wasn't doing me any good. But evidently it was or I couldn't have lived. Seemed like it wasn't. So they helped me outside. I went outside. I set down on a seat just outside. And naturally there was my wife and a bunch of them gathered around me, praying for me. So I sat there on that seat a little bit and I passed out. My boy said that my jaws locked. And he prized my jaws open.

"And the next thing I remember, Brother Preast was out there. And I heard him say, 'Jesus, rebuke this death spirit off Brother Turner.' I snapped back into the world. Then from then on I started getting a little better, but it wasn't nothing to brag about. So I laid down on the ground. Seemed like I wanted to be where I could get cold. So I laid down on the ground. And in a little bit I told him I was ready and I wanted to go

133

home. He said, 'Well, that's what I was waiting on to hear you say.' So they sent—now he was in his pick-up that night—so they sent down and got a quilt pad and rolled me over on it. I wasn't even able to get on it. They rolled me over on it to pack me down there, put me into the truck and took me home, packed me out of it and put me in my bed. So I started drinking water and—I don't know—pop, juices, first one thing and then another. Directly I started vomiting. When I vomited, why it looked like about half blood. So in a little bit this policeman come in.''

ELZIE PREAST: ''That night he was so bad, and after we got him to the house, this cop came there. And he shined his light down into a pan of blood where Brother Turner'd been spitting. And I thought, Lord, Lord, that is ugly. You have to put yourself back in a position before you got the Lord, Brother Ed, sometimes, to sympathize with people. And here this policeman shined his light down into that pan of blood and Brother Turner laying on the bed there, so sick and in as much pain as he was in. And the policeman shining his light down there in that pan. And he said, 'Joe, you're in bad—you're sick. Don't you think we ought to get you to a doctor? You're in pretty bad shape.'

''Brother Turner recognized who he was and he said, 'Don't bother me. I'll be all right. Just leave me alone.' ''

JOE TURNER: ''So I stayed in that bed about fourteen days and nights. And I went two days and nights and never slept a wink before I started to sleep. Didn't scarcely eat nothing. A few strawberries was about all I ate for several days.

''I was bit right here on the hand. Bit me right along here. All this hide come off from around here. All that peeled off right here. I had large blood blisters on my hand. See, it's still—see how the muscle is? Copperhead will make you real sick. I wouldn't say they couldn't kill you because they could. They'll make you wish you was dead, you'd be so sick. But a rattlesnake—what a rattlesnake does, it paralyzes you and busts your bloodstreams inside. You can hemorrhage to death, see. I'd say I went for—oh, I don't know—may fifteen or twenty days it put blood through my waterworks. Every time they'd take water, it'd look real dingy, bloodish-looking. Cause that's what they do, see? Busts you inside and causes you to hemorrhage to death.

''I believe really, if they'd took me to the hospital, I'd a died. Cause I felt I had every bit I could stand. Couldn't stand no more. I just felt I had all I could take. If I'd have went there, they'd have give me some of that medicine and that would have killed me. I believe that with all my heart. And I feel that they've been some of them died in the hospital with serpent bite—if they'd have stayed out and let the people pray for them, they wouldn't have died.

''I had a woman last summer got bit with one of my serpents and

dragon was cast out, that old serpent, called the

Lord, I want to be a Christian
in-a my heart
in-a my heart,
Lord, I want to be a Christian
in-a my heart.

Devil, and Satan which deceiveth the whole world:

Let Jesus come into your heart.
  Just now your doubtings give o'er,
  Just now, reject Him no more,
  Just now, throw open the door;
Let Jesus come into your heart.

he was cast out into the earth, and his angels

killed her. She lived a week. She got bit Saturday night down at Brother Dempsey's. And on Sunday her boy come in from out of state or something. So he didn't ask any questions. He just up and called an ambulance and took her to the hospital. And the following Sunday she died. So he goes around, you know, in the hospital, telling them he's the one saved his mother's life. He felt she was OK. She was going to get out. He's the one 'saved her life' you know. Well, if it hadn't been for him, she would have lived. And she died anyway. But they sent her to the hospital and naturally the church just let down with prayer. If you're going to trust in the arm of flesh, why you just go right ahead. So they just let down praying for her. I believe with all my heart, if they had left her down there where she was, she'd a been living today.

"I've heard the more you get bit the less it does to you, but—course Brother Preast has been bit—I don't know the times—around a dozen. And that last one he said bit him came near to killing him. When one even bit him, he prayed to die. I don't know. It's a great big something. Sometimes it just looks like it's according to your faith. The faith you've got. And a lot of times I think it's for—if somebody feels that we do something wrong, it's to prove to them maybe that we don't, see? I was bit one time right here in the side of the head with a rattlesnake. Didn't hurt me a bit. Just bled a lot. But it didn't hurt me a bit. I was bit on this finger one time. Got me on each side of my finger. That swelled up just a little bit. Just went like that. Then I was bit on this finger—I think by a copperhead. It swelled up my arm and spread. And this time with this rattlesnake. This is only three times it ever bothered me.

ELZIE PREAST: "It works on some of them breathing. It never did bother me too much in my breathing, but I've seen others that it did. But wherever it first bites you, it ain't that that really hurts. The bite. It's not like jabbing you with a pin or something, you know. The bite doesn't hurt you, but the aftereffects when that poison gets into your blood stream. Now rattlesnakes works more on your nerves or your breathing. It paralyzed Brother Turner, and like I say, I've seen others paralyzed. But copperheads—seem like it just works more on your bones. You just ache and hurt just like a—and it makes you deathly sick. I've been bit with both, but it seems like the rattlesnake poison works more on your nerves. You just feel like—seemed like I'd be so sleepy, I'd think, well I'm going to sleep, you see. And then something will just tear you up, and you're not going to sleep. It's your nerves. It'll be so much misery."

JOE TURNER: "I told my wife I certainly thank God for everybody that showed such a good love towards me. Brother Preast here and his wife. It really done something to me. Amen. And to feel that people would stay—glory to God—lose sleep and take time—Amen—and help you and do everything they can to give you a peaceful hour.

Bestow, dear Lord, upon our youth,
　The gift of saving grace;
And let the seed of sacred truth
　Fall in a fruitful place.

laid hold on the dragon, that old serpent,

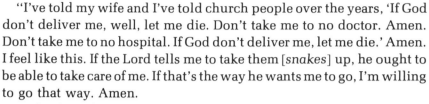

"I've told my wife and I've told church people over the years, 'If God don't deliver me, well, let me die. Don't take me to no doctor. Amen. Don't take me to no hospital. If God don't deliver me, let me die.' Amen. I feel like this. If the Lord tells me to take them [snakes] up, he ought to be able to take care of me. If that's the way he wants me to go, I'm willing to go that way. Amen.

"I thank God tonight for the serpent bite that I received. And if my hand stays like that, I'll thank God for it. I haven't anything to do but run the road and preach, noway that I know of. Amen. I thank God for it. I'm glad that it bit me. You say why? It learnt me a lot of things. I saw things that I never would have saw without it. And it brought me to have more love for people. And it helped me surely to acknowledge God's power. And since I've got serpent-bit, I couldn't tell you the messages I've preached in Charleston and different places that I've been in. So many people say, 'Oh, what's the matter with that hand?'

"And I come back, and I say, 'You probably wouldn't believe it, but I'll tell you. I got serpent-bit.' I've had so many talks with people no doubt I would have never probably got to mention the Bible to, especially lots of different business people that we've been around since we've got serpent-bit. And there's something about that hand that seems to attract people. They want to know what happened. It better gives me a chance to mention something to them about Jesus—glory to God. I thought it was a great advertisement. And I said a little while ago if God never does any more to it than just like it is, I'll walk and be happy. Ah, glory to God."

In churches where snakes are handled, other common practices include the drinking of strychnine, testing of faith by fire, and greeting in church with a "holy kiss."

While Joe Turner was still recovering from rattlesnake poisoning, he brought strychnine to church in a quart Mason Jar. He and others would drink from it several times during a service and seemed to suffer no ill effects.

ELZIE PREAST: "Now Brother Ed here used to bring strychnine to church. This brother sitting right here. He would mix up strychnine. Seemed to me like every time he come to church he had to have his strychnine. He was about as bad as a baby after its bottle, for strychnine—I think I can put it in them terms—but you see, it was worrying me. Maybe it wasn't bothering him at all. He wasn't, seemed like, paying much attention to it, and here he'd come every time. And he wouldn't stop with one time. He'd drink it two or three or maybe even more times in a service. And I thought, well, Lord, what in the world does he have to do that for all the time like that? And I got to worrying about it. And praying about it. Well, I found myself drinking

which is the Devil, and Satan, and bound him

By and by when the morning comes
    All the saints of God are gathering home,
We will tell the story how we overcome,
    We will understand it better by and by.

140

some after that. I never did like it that well, though, I'll tell the truth about it. And it's dangerous. It's bitter. It's deadly. It's been known to kill people. You say, 'Well, do you know somebody that's been killed?' Yeah, I sure do. It's not anything to play with. But it was just me worrying. That was my spirit, see? That was my worrying about it. I thank the Lord it's like it is."

In order to test their faith by fire, some worshipers at Elzie Preast's church in Scrabble Creek have held blowtorches to their faces or picked up hot coals without being burned. In the summer someone occasionally brings a blowtorch to church, and in winter the coals may be taken from the stove used for heating. The Biblical reference for this may be found in Hebrews 11:32-34, where the Apostle Paul tells of the prophets who through faith "quenched the violence of fire."

It is also from the writings of Paul (I Corinthians 16:20) that many Holiness churches in West Virginia and elsewhere find their instruction to "greet ye one another with an holy kiss." Even though some of his neighbors call it free love, JOE TURNER *tells his congregation:*

"I'm a firm believer—Amen—in greeting in church with a holy kiss, as the Bible says. Amen. It's the word of God to greet ye one another. People is so haughty in mind tonight and so up in society—there's some that comes here sometimes—and they preach it's wrong to wear a watch. It's wrong to wear a ring. And all the same time you can go to greet them, and they'll turn their head sideways to you like a billygoat. In other words, 'I don't believe in kissing tonight, neighbor.' And that lets me know that they don't know what they're preaching about. Ah, praise God, if they were that holy—weren't wearing jewelry or whatever—they would practice the rest of what the Lord said. It lets me know they don't know either.

"Let me tell you one thing tonight, neighbor. If you feel any evil over greeting some woman any more than you would some man, the devil is in you somewhere. The devil is in you somewhere. I don't think any more about these sisters than I would my dad and mother or about your little children, Brother Delbert. When it comes to anything evil whatsoever, in any way. Looky here. The Bible said the Holy Ghost thinketh no evil. Thinketh no evil. The Holy Ghost. And the Bible plainly said to greet ye one another with the holy kiss."

ELZIE PREAST: "Everybody don't agree with Brother Turner. But do you have to hang your head down because somebody thinks that you're not right? You know they look upon us as free lovers, and they look on us as snake handlers. Well, the best thing to do if you believe—is just get a sister up and kiss her. Or a brother, either one. That's the best way to prove to people you believe it. Just go on and enjoy yourself. Bless the

Lord. Why I wouldn't care tonight—glory to God—if the President of the United States was here. It wouldn't change my feeling one bit, glory to God. In fact, it might give me more power. The Lord might give me more power to tell him how he ought to do and how he ought to live. A lot of times, if people knew how to do, they could be better leaders of our country. I would count it a privilege tonight. I don't think I would be ashamed if I had the opportunity to be on television national and wide, and tell it to the whole United States and other countries, too, that Jesus is the King of Glory and that the Holy Ghost is from God out of heaven. Bless the Lord!"

with an holy kiss. (I CORINTHIANS 16:20)

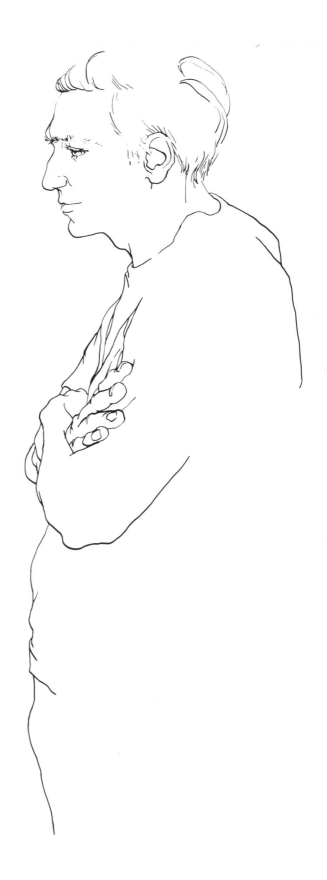

Amazing grace, how sweet the sound,
    That saved a wretch like me!
I once was lost, but now I'm found;
    Was blind, but now I see.

And he said, A certain man had two sons: And

In the cross, in the cross,
Be my glory ever;
Till my raptured soul shall find
Rest beyond the river.

The Black Prodigal

First Calvary Baptist Church is located in an integrated urban neighborhood in Knoxville, Tennessee. The brick building is well kept and the congregation, predominately black, is a stable and close-knit group. They have been praying and singing together for many years. When the **REVEREND J.M.KIMBALL,** *on leave from a nearby church, held a revival at First Calvary the response was enthusiastic. His only difficulty lay in finding as much as one lost soul for the mourners' bench.*

REVEREND KIMBALL: To my friend and your pastor, the Reverend Charles W. Matthews, to the membership of First Calvary, the utmost respect to each of you gathered here. And a double respect goes to this great choir. And maybe you could say Amen for them, too.

CONGREGATION: Amen.

REVEREND KIMBALL: For they have done a good job.

CONGREGATION: Yes. Yes.

REVEREND KIMBALL: Including their proficient musicians. For that's where it's happening.

CONGREGATION: Yes, yes.

REVEREND KIMBALL: We are here this week at your pastor's request —and am—your pastor for this week. That just means that I am an evangelist that he has imported to carry on with you. And I tell you, there's no reason why we shouldn't have a good time!

Christian Friends, a revival has two avenues. Now, I'm used to somebody saying Amen.

CONGREGATION: Amen.

REVEREND KIMBALL: I say a revival has two avenues. Namely: to revive up. And to touch the untouched and to reach the unreached and to convert the unconverted. To me a revival is a noisy meeting. Do I hear a noise?

CONGREGATION: Amen.

REVEREND KIMBALL: To me a revival is a noisy meeting. You can't just do it quietly. You've got to make a joyful noise. And yet sometimes we have secret prayers—and that is necessary—but I swear unto you, we ought to make a joyful noise.

CONGREGATION: Amen.

REVEREND KIMBALL: It's your job and mine to make the world better. And the only way that we can make the world better, we'll have to convert the world. We'll have to church the unchurched.

Yes.

We'll have to reach the unreached.

Yes.

And we'll have to make the unconcerned concerned.

Amen.

give me the portion of goods that falleth to me.

You've got to make people believe that you're serving the right God.

        Amen.

You know, you just got to act like that.

        Yes.

You got to talk the talk you talk.

        Yes.

And you've got to walk the walk you walk.

        Yes.

And you've got to live the life you sing about.

        Amen.

Often, in both black and white churches, a preacher's message is punctuated by cries of Amen, Hallelujah, or Praise the Lord. But as Reverend Kimball continues, supported by responses from the congregation, his entire sermon becomes a kind of musical chant. It is thought that many of the hymns now sung by various denominations were "composed" in this manner during the camp meetings of the early 1800s. Indeed, the preacher and the congregation were virtually singing through most of the following sermon, Reverend Kimball's version of the Parable of the Prodigal Son. At first he begins slowly. The responses of the congregation are murmurs. But as the story builds, so does the excitement and the tempo of the chant. Before it is finished, the congregation is dancing in the aisles as they follow the prodigal son on his journey.

REVEREND KIMBALL: Christian friends, tonight the Lord would have it be that we are going to try to share with you what is in our hearts. And to have a guideline, we have deemed it necessary to deal with Dr. Luke —that we call St. Luke.

        Oh yes.

Amen.

        Amen.

The physician that healeth the delicate minister, the greatest missionary the world has ever known, Brother Paul. Great Dr. Luke was his doctor.

        Oh yes.

Amen.

        Oh yes.

But we want to deal here with Dr. Luke tonight. And we want to bother with the fifteenth chapter and use as our discourse its eighteenth verse. And will you listen, if you please. "I will arise—"

        Yes, yes.

"And go to my father."

        Yes.

"And will say unto him,"

        Yes. Amen.

And he divided unto them his living. And not

O Mary, don't you weep, don't you mourn,
O Mary, don't you weep, don't you mourn;
Pharoh's army got drowned,
O Mary, don't you weep.

many days after the younger son gathered all

Tell me where can I go?
Tell me where can I go?
Tell me where can I go?
      In the country? He's there.
      In the valley? He's there.
      In my home? He's there.
      In the dark? He's there.
Nowhere, nowhere, nowhere can you go but to the Lord.

"Father, I have sinned"
        Yes.
"Against Heaven"
        Yes.
"And before thee,"
        Yes, yes.
"And am no more worthy—"
        No more worthy.
"To be called thy son:"
        Amen.
"Make me as one of thy hired servants."
        Yes, all right.
You know it?
        Yes. Amen.
Our theme tonight—and you may not even agree with me—
        Oh, yes.
But here is the theme: I am on my way!
        On my way!
To my father's house.
        Yes, yes.
And I'm going to visit him.
        Yes, yes.
And I'm not going to visit anybody else.
        Oh yes.
But I'm on my way.
        Yes. Amen.
To *my* father's house.
        Yes, yes.
See, if I come to your father's house or go to your father's house, I might need a formal invitation.
        Yes.
But I can go *home* when I get ready.
        Yes. Oh yes. Amen.
We have organized Brother Hale that's in the choir to cooperate with us tonight. When we get the Prodigal Son underway, we want to bring him home. And to keep you from being excited when we bring him home, we have a robe for him.
        Oh yes.
And to keep him from being too disturbed, we have a ring in my pocket for him.
        Oh yes. Amen. Amen.
You see, a lot of people expect we're going to put on a stunt.
        Oh no. Amen.
But I want you to hear what we're going to do.
        Oh yes.

and there wasted his substance with riotous

So you will not be surprised.
        Amen.
When my son comes home.
        Yes. Yes.
The Bible says there was a certain man.
        Yes.
That had two sons.
        Yes. Right.
The Lord said a certain man.
        Yes.
He didn't say Mr. Jones.
        No.
He didn't say Mr. Smith.
        No.
He didn't say Mr. Walker.
        No.
He didn't say Mr. White.
        No.
But he said a certain man.
        Yes.
You better hear me now.
        Oh yes.
He had two sons.
        Yes.
You have to go along with me.
        Yes, yes.
Yes, this man must have been a pretty good liver.
        Yes.
This man must have been good of character.
        Yes.
This man was not henpecked.
        Yes.
Any man
        Yes?
That lets a woman push him around,
        Yes, yes.
Or any man that has to take all the information
        Yes.
That enables him to talk
        Yes.
From a woman—
        Yes.
Is henpecked.
        Yes, yes.

living. (LUKE 15:11-13)   I will arise and go to my

I am bound for the Promised Land,
I am bound for the Promised Land,
O who will come and go with me?
I am bound for the Promised Land.

I'll trust in the blood,
I'll trust in the blood,
    The blood that was offered for sin to atone,
I'll trust in the blood,
The life giving blood,
    That flows from the side of the Crucified One.

sinned against heaven, and before thee. And am

And any man that can't tell his wife
                    Yes. Great!
What he wants her to know,
                    Yes.
And has to send word to her
                    Yes.
By the neighbor next door—is henpecked!
                    Yes, yes. Great! Great!
I know this man was not henpecked.
                    No, no.
This man was a full man.
                    Yes.
This man
                    Yes.
Was a full-fledged man.
                    Yes.
This man
                    Yes.
Was a good provider
                    Yes.
For the household.
                    Yes.
In his home he had a long table,
                    Yes.
And in his kitchen he had plenty of food.
                    Yes, yes.
You better listen to me.
                    Yes.
And in his treasury he had plenty of money.
                    Yes.
And in his heart
                    Yes.
He had plenty love.
                    Yes.
And in his head
                    Yes.
He had plenty of sense.
                    Yes.
And on his mind
                    Yes.
He had plenty gumption.
                    Yes.
That's plenty gumption. You all listen to me.
                    Yes.

You got to go that lonesome valley,
You got to go there by yourself;
O nobody else can do it for you,
You got to go there all alone.

one of thy hired servants. And he arose, and came

Where is my wand'ring boy tonight—
The boy of my tend'rest care,
The boy that was once my joy and light,
The child of my love and prayer?

And in his eyes he had long sight.
> Yes.
And in his feet
> Yes.
He had long steps.
> Yes.
And on his shoulders he had broadness.
> Yes. Great!
And under the old tradition
> Yes.
It was expected
> Yes.
That the older son
> Yes, yes.
Would get married first.
> Yes. Oh yes.
So it was expected
> Yes.
That the oldest son
> Oh, yes.
Would have left home first.
> Yes,
But he should have looked at the youngest son.
> Yes, yes.
You people now, you got to follow me.
> Yes, great! Great!
The youngest son with a prayer in his heart.
> Yes.
The youngster was a little skeptical.
> Yes.
We have wide mouths, then, my friends.
> Yes.
They will ask you by one word—
> Yes.
For three thousand dollars.
> Yes.
And then he'll say, "Dad—"
> Yes.
"May I use the car tonight?"
> Yes, yes.
And won't even scratch his head.
> Yes, yes.
And you, my friend—
> Yes, yes. Great!

Will let your son have the car.
>Yes.

You'll lend him three thousand dollars.
>Yes.

Sometimes four and five thousand you might lend him.
>Yes, yes.

So the youngest son kept looking at his father and trying to make up enough—to get enough gumption in his mind—and enough grit in his craw, to ask his father a favor.
>Yes.

And one day
>Um-hmmm.

He walked up to his father.
>Yes.

He said, "Father, give me my portion. The portion of goods that falleth to me."
>Yes.

And his father looked at the boy.
>Yes.

And his father understood.
>Yes.

And so his father gave him
>Yes.

The portion of the goods that fell to him.
>Yes.

And suddenly he got kind of quiet,
>Yes.

Just for one moment.
>Yes. Great!

And then he seen
>Yes.

That the youngest son
>Yes.

Was packing up,
>Yes.

Getting ready to go.
>Yes.

Packing up,
>Yes.

Getting ready to go.
>Yes, yes.

Packing up.
>Yes.

Getting ready to go.
>Yes.

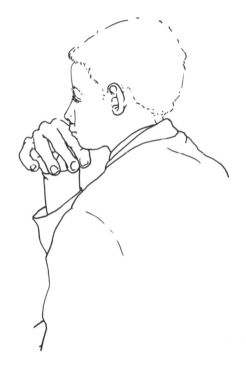

off, his father saw him, and had compassion, and

EZEKIEL 22:30.
AND I SOUGHT
FOR A MAN AM-
ONG THEM, THAT
SHOULD MAKE UP
THE HEDGE, AND
STAND IN THE GAP
BEFORE ME FOR
THE LAND, THAT I
SHOULD NOT DE-
STROY IT; BUT I
FOUND NONE

Packing up,
        Yes.
Getting ready to go.
        Yes.
Packing up, getting ready to go.
        Yes, yes.
And then his father reached somewhere in his pocket.
        Yes, yes.
And the son starts moving.
        Yes.
Moving.
        Yes.
Moving.
        Yes.
Moving.
        Yes.
Moving, moving.
        Yes, yes, yes.
Moving.
        Yes.
Moooooving.
        Yes, yes.
Hallelujah!
        Yes.
Hallelujah, Amen.
        Yes.
When he got to the first town—
        Yes.
When he got to the first town, he said, "I can't stop here."
        Yes.
"My father's a full-fledged citizen."
        Yes.
"And everybody knows"
        Yes.
"All around"
        Yes.
"The news."
        Yes. The news (*shouting and clapping*)!
"So I can't stop here."
        Yes.
"My father's known"
        Yes.
"In this little town."
        Yes.

ran, and fell on his neck, and kissed him. And

What a friend we have in Jesus,
All our sins and griefs to bear;
What a privilege to carry
Ev'rything to God in prayer.

the son said unto him, Father, I have sinned

He kept moving.
> Yes.

Moving.
> Yes.

Moving.
> Yes, moving.

And when he got to the next town,
> Yes.

He said, "I can't stop here. My father's well known."
> Yes.

"I got to go moving."
> Yes.

"Moving, to a far country."
> Yes.

Moving.
> Yes, yes (*clapping and shouting*)!

Moving to a far country.
> Yes.

And when he got to the far country,
> Yes.

He had a well-rounded room.
> Yes.

And he was able to change clothes every day.
> Yes.

And one night—
> Yes.

He went down to the corner
> Yes.

And stood
> Yes.

And said to those, "Where do the boys hang out?"
> Yes, yes?

And somebody told him the boys were hanging out
> Yes.

In the redlight district.
> Yes!

By this time the excitement had built to such a pitch that it was impossible to record individuals speaking. Reverend Kimball led the robed "prodigal" down the aisle, around the church, and back again followed by many of the congregation. They danced and clapped their hands. Some began speaking in tongues.

Throughout the week, Reverend Kimball continued his theme of coming home "to my father's house."

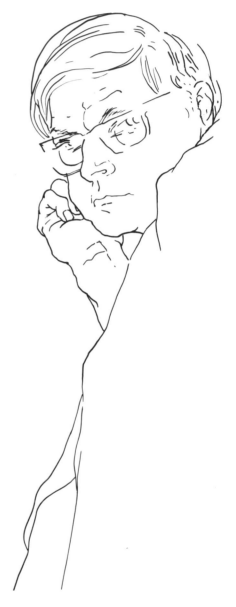

REVEREND KIMBALL: I have a feeling that somebody ought to join the church tonight. Somebody that's not attached ought to join.

      Yes. Amen.

Somebody that never has been a member of a church ought to join.

      Yes, yes.

Or somebody ought to deem it necessary to choose First Calvary as his church home. Is there anybody—

      Yes.

That has ever been in trouble? Is there anybody here

      Yes.

That has a burden on your shoulders?

      Yes.

Is there anybody here

      Yes.

That has been mistreated?

      Yes.

Is there anybody here

      Yes, yes.

That has ever been out at night

      Yes, yes.

In the cold alone?

      Yes, yes.

I don't have any weapons, but I can open a door for you.

      Yes.

He can open a door for you.

      Yes, yes.

Is there anybody here

      Yes, yes.

That's ever gotten lonesome?

      Yes, yes.

I want to search them out tonight.

      Yes.

If you're out of the church

      Yes.

You ought to come home.

      Yes.

While the wind

      Yes.

Is still blowing,

      Yes.

You ought to come home.

      Yes.

While the sun is still shining on everything,

      Yes.

Where is my wandering boy tonight!
    Down in the licensed saloon.
Learning new vices all the night long,
    Tempted to all that's sinful and wrong,
Listening to the harlot's foul song,
    Down in the licensed saloon.

more worthy to be called thy son. But the

Will the circle be unbroken
By and by, by and by?
In a better home a-waiting,
In the sky, in the sky?

father said to his servants, Bring forth the best

Come by here, my Lord
Come by here
Come by here, my Lord
Come by here
O Lord, Come by here.

robe, and put it on him; and put a ring on his

You ought to come home.
>Yes.

While God is still on his throne, you ought to come home.
>Yes.

You come on and join us. I'm going to sing for you tonight. You needn't help unless you want to.
>Yes!

Reverend Kimball began singing "Give Me a Home," but the hymn was interrupted again and again by cries of "Come on!" "Join the church!" until at last one woman came forward. Incidentally, the procedure of voting into membership (though interrogation may be handled differently) is a formality practiced in all Baptist churches.

REVEREND KIMBALL: Do you believe that Jesus Christ is the son of the living God? Do you accept him now as your Savior?

WOMAN: Yes.

REVEREND KIMBALL: Jesus said, "If you own me before man, I'll own you before my father."

CONGREGATION: Yes!

REVEREND KIMBALL: This sister has come into our church as a candidate for baptism. All who will vote to receive this sister as a candidate for baptism and extend the right hand of fellowship—and then she'll have all the rights of the church—prepare to vote. All in favor, let's say Amen!

CONGREGATION: Amen! Amen!

REVEREND KIMBALL: Do you have a word that you'd like to say?

WOMAN: I know that I've saved my soul.

CONGREGATION: Yes, yes.

WOMAN: I've saved it!

The woman was weeping as she responded. The others shouted and clapped.

REVEREND KIMBALL: Lord, receive this sister as a candidate for baptism, giving her the right hand of fellowship.

CONGREGATION: Amen. Amen.

REVEREND KIMBALL: Bless you. Thank God. We prayed for this soul. We mourned for this soul. We thought once we wasn't going to get it.
>Yes.

God always knows the way.
>Yes.

I thank God for this soul. I feel good.
>Yes.

I'm revived tonight.
>Yes.

hand, and shoes on his feet. (LUKE 15:18-22)

Being revived makes me feel good.
>Yes, yes.

Keep on praying.
>Yes, yes.

I want to talk about something that I know.
>Oh yes.

And it's black language.
>Yes. Oh yes.

You know, we folks use—
>Yes. Oh yes (*shouting*)!

We have tried to get away from our dialect.
>Yeah man.

Black is beautiful.
>Yes.

And our language is good.
>Yes. Hallelujah!

It's all right to go to school. But don't you show out.
>Yes, yes.

Be what you are.
>Amen.

I'm going to take my chances and serve my Lord.
>Yes, yes.

Because my Lord is color-blind.
>Yes. Amen.

He does not differentiate between black and white.

And the gospel must first be published among all

A Ministry of Sign Painting

On the opening night of REVIVAL! in Washington, after a gala dinner party and the festivities at the Corcoran Gallery, Eleanor Dickinson led a small group to Lookout Point on the Potomac River. The director, curators, and other staff members of the Corcoran came along, as well as the artist's mother, husband, and a number of friends. Everyone sang "Onward, Christian Soldiers" and took turns hurling pint whiskey bottles into the Potomac. Each bottle was tightly corked and contained a religious message instead of whiskey. By this time it was late, but the night was still hot and muggy. Several young people dressed in dungarees were asleep on the grass. Some awakened and stared incredulously, but Dickinson refused to allow anyone to stop singing or throwing bottles. "It's part of the total art form," she insisted. "Besides, I promised Brother Mayes."

Brother Mayes is Harrison Mayes of Middlesboro, Kentucky. He is an evangelist who has never in his life preached a sermon, but if you drive along the highways, particularly in the South and West, you can see his religious signs. They are usually just off the right-of-way and placed so that they can be easily seen by passing motorists. They may be aluminum on a wooden frame. Some of the largest are cast in concrete and weigh fourteen hundred pounds. They are almost always in the shape of a cross, and the red and blue letters tell you to GET RIGHT WITH GOD or that JESUS IS COMING SOON.

You may well have seen his airport signs also. These are usually placed at the end of the runway, so that as your plane takes off you can look down and read PREPARE TO MEET GOD. In addition to his sign painting, Brother Mayes searches the streets of Middlesboro for empty whiskey bottles. Then he and his wife carefully wash them and insert the message, translated into fourteen languages. Most of the translating has been done at the University of Tennessee, and Brother Mayes is still praying for the University of Tennessee foreign language departments. Each bottle is numbered, so that he will know how long it has been in the water. One was put in the Pacific off the coast of South America and turned up in the Philippines sixteen years later. Another crossed the Atlantic from Long Island to England. Since the opening of REVIVAL! Eleanor Dickinson has also thrown Brother Mayes's bottles into New York Harbor and San Francisco Bay. She promised him she would, in exchange for his giving her several signs to display with her drawings.

There are other religious sign painters but Brother Mayes is certainly the most active, with signs in all fifty states and eighty-two foreign countries. The ones for foreign countries are painted on plastic (he has recently begun using fluorescent paint), then neatly rolled and inserted

165

in mailing tubes. He was working at this when the artist drew his portrait. These plastic signs are later mounted on boards by missionaries. Local churches supply him with their names and addresses. In 1952 he sent a sign directly to Joseph Stalin; however, he never received a reply.

His largest sign measures 105 feet. It's electric and situated on top of a mountain just outside of Middlesboro. **BROTHER MAYES** *pays the electric bill himself, but complains, "They've got so many trees set down out there right close to it, you can't hardly see it."*

Brother Mayes worked in the Kentucky coal mines for many years, but always spent his vacations traveling across the country installing his signs. "Lord have mercy!" he exclaimed when asked how far he had traveled. "I've made enough mileage to go around the earth ten times, I guess." Now retired, he makes the money to carry on his religious work by painting signs for a soft drink company and also a firm that makes trailer trucks. From the truck manufacturer he gets aluminum at a discount.

"The Lord's running this machine, and when I need money I can make it just as easy. It takes a lot of money to carry on. I don't need any money, see. I'm retired on Social Security and pension—miners' pension and this black lung. Me and my wife live on that. All I make, I put it back into the work of the Lord, all of it. Me and Sister Mayes draws a little over three hundred dollars a month. We don't owe nobody or nothing. We got our own place to live here. That gives me and her a chance just to work for the Lord. She goes to church all the time, and I go on the highway all the time. There's not a man living on this earth that's had any more heartaches than I've had in fifty-two years of carrying this work on. But turn it right over, there's nobody had any more happiness than I've had doing it.

"If you have everything easy, you just get to where you're not worth anything. For a sample I was up here at Raleigh-Durham Airfield last week. I put a sign up there at that airfield. Well, I got down to the west end approach. Well, then there's this farmhouse. It was too far away, but I was aiming to put it there anyway. And I told her what I was doing—the lady—and she said, 'Now that racket has been in here before.' I'd had a sign pretty close there for years, you know, up till they lengthened the field out and had to tear it down. Well, she just kept on, 'Racket! Racket!'

"I said, 'Now listen. Now this is not a racket. Now I'm a-telling you now, and I mean this for the good of man.'

"Well, she just went right up then, just as good as to say, 'You better get yourself away from here right now.' Well, I did. I went down to the—out and down to the east approach and found the best place that ever I put a sign since I been putting signs around the airfields. So she

was published throughout all the region.

We need a whole lot more of Jesus
and a lot less rock and roll

How beautiful upon the mountains

Work, for the night is coming;
Work, through the morning hours;
Work, for the night is coming,
When man's work is done.

didn't know she was a-blessing me by blessing me out. I've got twenty-five or thirty at these airfields [*at such varied locations as Chicago, Atlanta, and West Palm Beach*] but I've had some torn down. Had three torn down right here at Knoxville. The airlines tore them down. They're afraid of disturbing their passengers, and then they come in here fussing about trash being down there at the end of the runway. I know what I'm doing—disturbing their passengers."

In his backyard workshop Brother Mayes keeps road maps of most of the United States, carefully marked with the locations of his signs.

"You've got to know what you're doing. I've got there at the back there practically all the states' rules and regulations. You've just simply got to know what you're doing or you're just losing all your signs.

"The masses of traffic is on the Interstate, and I've been laying off of them up until last year. I'll show you how I work it. They've asked everybody to keep 660 feet away from this fence on the Interstate. I can't do that. It's too far, and I've got to make a sign too big. I can't stand it. I'm a part of this United States. And there's freedom of religion, speech, and the press, but it don't mean you can get out and put a sign where somebody'll get killed with it. So long as you've got freedom, you've got to use horse sense with it. If I get out and put up a sign where somebody will get hurt, I ought to be put in jail. Here's the way I do this. Right here comes the Interstate. Now here's the fence. In other words, the Interstate fence. There's a little old road coming up through here to Farmer Brown's. Maybe he lives up here someplace. Here's his fence. His fence and his land right here. Then here is this old road, and that's gone back to the county. I call that no-man's land. The only way you can do, if a man rolls up on you—he's got only five minutes to catch me, cause I'm putting that sign together right there in the truck. My buddy's digging the hole up there. State man come along, and he thinks Farmer Brown's putting something up up there. Farmer Brown comes along, he'll think the state's a-putting something up there. When I get that hole dug and that sign together, then I bring it right up there and stick it down in that hole, and he's got five minutes to catch me. I'm gone.

Brother Mayes showed Eleanor Dickinson a letter he had recently received from the Ohio State Police, informing him that since his signs were on the right-of-way they were illegal and would have to be removed.

"They're on the right-of-way. Well, I knowed that. You see, there was five of them. And he told me right where they're at. Well, I know they're on the right-of-way because I can't do nothing else. I get them just as near the right-of-way as I can get. So that's the size of it right there. Now that man, he's doing his duty. I'm a-doing mine. And what we got to do is to work it out.

"And I told him what to do with it. Leave them stay there till—as long as possible—or till I can pick them up. Well, I'm not picking them up. I'm being back in five years, but he don't know that. I didn't say that. I said, 'Leave them as long as you can or till I can pick them up. And if you have to take them down before I can pick them up, why you have Farmer Brown set it back, just a foot.' They're all within a foot of the right-of-way. 'Set it back, just on Farmer Brown's place and send me a bill for five dollars for just setting it back. Or get some man that's retired and wants to make him twenty-five dollars for setting them five back. Why, just set them back and send me a bill, and I'll send him twenty-five dollars. Or, if you have to take them up, why, take them down to the state garage where you're going to put them for me to pick up in thirty days—after thirty days—and set them up there where people can read them.' They'll do that. They'll help you out. I say, 'Help me any way you can because it costs me too much money.' Them cost me thirty-three dollars apiece. A thousand dollars is what that truckload of signs cost. Two thousand dollars for these two truckloads, and now this next one a-coming up—I'll show you—is another thousand dollars. Three thousand dollars this year.

"For a sample, I put one up here just this side of Yellowstone on this last trip. Well, I hadn't been back two days till I heard from a state man out there. He said, 'I took your sign down due to this here beautification that Mrs. Johnson signed into law. It's my duty to do it. I hate to do it.'

"Well, I wrote him back, and I said, 'Well now, I'm going to bless you out just a little bit in the name of the Lord because—now there ain't no kind of a sign nowhere that's any more appropriate or beautiful stuck alongside the road, out of the way, then a sign that reads GET RIGHT WITH GOD and then inviting people to come to church in that area. There ain't nothing any more beautiful than that.'"

Brother Mayes has all but discontinued the use of concrete for his highway signs, since aluminum is easier to handle and he can carry more signs in a truck at once. The large concrete crosses in the photograph on page 173 stand in the Mayes' backyard, but they are reserved for more distant locations.

"Now, I'm getting—I've got some made out there—them concrete ones—for the planets. For a sample, Jupiter and Mars and Venus. I'd say within twenty years they'll be taking bulldozers up there and everything else. And jet loads—I don't know what kind of a jet—of people. Maybe it would be possible that they'd have to have gas masks or something. I don't know how. The planet Jupiter—maybe when we enter the planet Jupiter we may start living forever, because they may

# of good, that publisheth salvation; that saith unto

Let the lower lights be burning!
Send a gleam across the wave:
Some poor fainting, struggling seaman;
You may rescue, you may save.

Zion, Thy God reigneth! (ISAIAH 52:7) Heaven

not have transgressed the laws of God like Adam did. We're going to leave here because we've transgressed. But they may not. I don't know that. I believe as much as I'm a-setting here that thousands and millions of what we call stars is inhabited. Cause there's a hundred million visible from this earth in this galaxy, much less the rest of them that's got life on them. We don't know that. Now the moon, it's highly possible that the moon has done exactly what this earth's going to do if we don't do something about this pollution. It's going to be a question of, well—I don't know how many years, but in the future, why there'll be nothing—grass nor nothing else'll grow and this will be a barren place. No life, no nothing, automatically. And that's what happened on the moon to my opinion.

"So these planets, I want to get some signs on them. We're going to have to get more speed than we've got though, if we get anywhere towards getting to the planets, because twenty-six million miles is as close as you can get to Mars from the earth. That's the closest you can get. They'll do it. By the year 1980 they figure they can get loads of passengers up to the moon. Going to the moon is a small thing. When you undertake to go to Mars, now, that's different."

In order to make sure that each of his signs reaches its destination, he has given his sons and grandsons the names of continents and planets. James S. America Mayes will have the job of transporting a concrete cross to South America; Clide Europe Mayes and Warren W. Indies Mayes also have their work cut out for them. But even more difficult tasks lie ahead for Jeff Uranus, Charles Pluto, Ronny Jupiter, Rickey Mercury, and the other young Mayes grandchildren. Brother Mayes, however, doesn't expect them to get started until some time in the 1990s. "I put it off that far," he says, "so I wouldn't have to fool with it."

"Now I better tell you about that little sign I got down at Cape Kennedy. Before the first flight to the moon, I fixed one three feet tall. Weighs six pounds. Sent it down there to the manager of the Cape—to set it up on the moon. Well, he wrote me back and said everything is dangerous and everything, and they hadn't even got there, you know, yet. And they were afraid to fool with it. I wrote him back and told him, I said, 'Well, set it up down there someplace where everybody can see it.' "

These two concrete crosses now stand on either side of the entrance to the Mayes' front walk in Middlesboro. But on the Day of Judgement one is to be erected on the banks of the Jordan River in the New Jerusalem and the other on the shores of hell. Since the photograph was taken, Mrs. Mayes has planted shrubbery in front of the cross destined for the shores of hell. She was afraid it might frighten the neighborhood children.

and earth shall pass away: but my words shall

The Mayes home is built in the shape of a cross. GET RIGHT WITH GOD is printed in large letters on the roof for the benefit of passing airplanes. The top of the house has twelve windows, representing the twelve apostles, and the lower half has ten—the Ten Commandments. The lot on which the house stands has twelve corners, each marked by a post, one for each of the twelve disciples. Eleven of the posts are concrete, but one is of wood. "That represents Judas," Brother Mayes explains. "I stole that post, cause I didn't want nothing good about it."

When Eleanor Dickinson arrived for one of her interviews, she found **MRS. MAYES** *seated on the front porch stringing "shuck beans." These are picked when green, strung in bunches, and hung in the sun to dry. Later they will hang in the attic for use during the winter. Mrs. Mayes also cans vegetables from the large garden beside the house, and during both winter and summer months the produce from the Mayes' garden is always shared with their neighbors.*

"They'll say, 'Well, I'm not a-going to help people because they're drawing Social Security. And they're drawing state aid.' The point of it is that that's starvation living. They're not having enough for nothing, after all. So we should go along there and help them anyway. And folks don't look at it thataway. They say, 'I'm not going to help them because they're getting a check, too.' But when you come right down to business they're not having enough to eat. All right, after we live and keep everything up, there's not but a little bit left. You just think about a man that's got four or five kids. If he's drawing a hundred and fifty dollars, what can he have? Just a cornbread living, that's all. And it's up to me to help somebody like that."

BROTHER MAYES *began working in the mines, where his father had worked before him, when he was fifteen.* "Spent all my life in the mines, the coal mines, about seven miles from here.

"There's hardly any of these deep mines a-running. Just a few now and then, but there is a lot of stripping. Oh, there used to be twenty-one mines up this branch right here and up this one. Now I believe there is one small one—or two—deep mines. That's all. They're not doing any good. The one that I worked at worked about three hundred men—three hundred and fifty—something like that. Now there's one or two—well, I'd say there's five houses up there. I remember when there was hundreds of them up there before, where we lived.

"It's awful dangerous; nearly everywhere you look in a deep coal mine it's dangerous. But all this here stripping coal—it's well, I'd say it's not as good as it is to go under there because it's been exposed to the weather outside, outcroppings and everything. Stripping all over this country just ruins the land. You take a hill this steep right here. And

then you plow this off here. How in the world are you going to get dirt back there right? You can't fill it. You might fudge at it, but that's all."

Brother Mayes was working in the mines when he first began to write religious messages, sometimes on a piece of slate.

"And I used to get me a tablet and write on it—you know we didn't have much money back then and there wasn't none to get, much —fifty-two years ago. I'd just get me a tablet and write out whatever I wanted to and tack it on a telephone pole and kept coming on up till I've got it to hundreds now—all these out of aluminum. It's just like a man preaching. He gets converted and—maybe he don't feel like he ought to do it—testifies. It puts them over the first time. Stage frights them, you know. First thing you know, he's talking a little bit. Next thing you know, you couldn't stop him with a maul. You couldn't stop Brother Roger Powell with nothing. Now he'll preach or bust. And that's the way it is. The only way you could stop me from putting up signs is to cut my throat. That's all."

*It was **REV. ROGER POWELL** who first told Eleanor Dickinson how to find his friend, Harrison Mayes. During the years he worked as a truck driver Reverend Powell made several trips across the country with Brother Mayes, driving truckloads of signs and helping to install them.*

REV. ROGER POWELL: "Actually, this thing with him is beyond the natural man. It's the supernatural, all right. And it's working through the man, just like it is in me praying for the sick. I'm just a man. But if I put my hands on him and a fellow gets well, that's more than a man. That's the way it is. And so he's got the directions on putting those signs up, just the same as I have getting a text to preach from it, or a verse of scripture, see? He has the same thing. It's a—he's got his directions. He can tell you right where it ought to be. He's got it in his mind right where they're going to be before he leaves home—about where they're going to set. He can just about pinpoint them, just about where they'll be, and he knows what he's doing—he knows."

While Reverend Powell discussed Harrison Mayes he was looking at the REVIVAL! drawings. "You're into something that's interesting. But it has to be given. That's right. You have to have this in you. Something has to get in you to bring this forward. You got to get the vision of it.

"It's beyond you. If it wasn't beyond you—if you could explain it—why, it would be artificial. But it's beyond you. You see, in other words, all you can do now is just use the simplicity of it to bring it out. In other words, it's a simple thing. It's simple, and it's so simple you can't afford to explain it. Because if you did, you'd explain it away.

"This I consider a great thing. You would not have got the vision of it if it hadn't a been given you. You just—if you'd been going to work for

not by constraint, but willingly . . .(I PETER 5:2)

the enemy, you'd a got a different vision. I'll tell you that right now. That's right.

"The Holy Ghost is an unseen person. It's the third person in the Godhead. And it's to work within us for the benefit of the people. It's not just something to brag about. It'll do its own advertising. It's the truth. That's right. But it's good to publish it. And great are them that publish this thing, see? I think you're doing a great work. Publish good tidings. If this would be of benefit to one person down the line somewhere, wouldn't it be worth it?

"Bless your heart. God bless you in your work."

Blessed is he that readeth, and they that hear

On the closing night of his revival at the Scott Street Assembly of God in Knoxville, Tennessee, **REV. JOE M. MILES** *offered this prayer:*

Now at this time we're going to have a special prayer.
This lady's been here with us night after night drawing these pictures.
She's going to exhibit these pictures in art galleries.
She's using this as a means to touch someone for the Lord.
They might be a means of winning someone to God.
So I'd like for us to pray a special prayer tonight over this art that she's
   been drawing, over this program that she's going to put forth in these
   art galleries, to try to touch someone with the gospel of the Lord
   Jesus Christ.
I think it's a wonderful effort, and wonderful thing, and wonderful
   opportunity.
We've got to use every means available to us to get the gospel—the
   Good News—out to the world.
So let's raise our hands and pray over these arts tonight.
Dear Heavenly Father, we pray that thou would go with these pictures
   into these art galleries.
Thy blessings be upon these drawings, that they might reach the heart
   of some boy, some man, some woman, some girl, over this universe
   of ours.
That they may stop—that they may recognize—they may begin to think
   that there is a God in Heaven.
A God who cares and understands.
And they might realize that there's a God who has the answer to the
   earth's sorrow and prayer.
Bless them, Heavenly Father God tonight.
In Jesus Christ's own name we pray forevermore.
Amen.
Amen.

Glossary

ALTAR CALL. Invitation to come forward to the mourners' bench, confess sins, and repent.

CASTING OUT DEVILS. Praying for a person believed to be possessed by devils. Being possessed may cause one to be ill or to be "mean and lustful."

FAITH HEALING. Praying for the sick with the expectation of immediate healing if faith in God is strong enough.

FOOTWASHING. The washing of one another's feet in a gesture of humility, as Christ washed his disciples' feet on the eve of his crucifixion.

HOLY KISS. Kissing one another in church in accordance with St. Paul's instruction: "Greet ye one another with an holy kiss."

LAYING-ON-OF-HANDS. The preacher and members of the congregation who are saved place their hands on the head of the penitent so that the Holy Ghost can enter through them—may be used for the purpose of healing or casting out devils.

MOURNERS' BENCH. A bench—or three or four chairs—placed at the front of the tent or church and turned to face the congregation. Here the penitent come to kneel and pray for forgiveness of their sins.

NINE GIFTS. The Nine Gifts of the Holy Ghost, healing, speaking in tongues, prophecy, etc., as outlined by St. Paul in his first epistle to the Corinthians.

PRAYER CLOTH. A cloth prayed over by the preacher and anointed with oil. Believed by some to have healing powers. Often sent to a person too ill to come to a revival service.

PROPHESYING. While in a trancelike state the individual speaks in the first person, as if God were speaking through him.

REVIVAL. An evangelical service or series of services, specifically held to effect a religious awakening. A revival may last for days or weeks and may be held in a church or open tent.

SPEAKING IN TONGUES. Speaking in an unintelligible language, believed to be a sign that one is possessed by the Holy Ghost. Also called Glossolalia. It occurs many times in the Bible and is one of the Pentecostal phenomena that has lately emerged in many denominations.

TESTIFYING. Members of the congregation stand and speak, usually to bear witness to what God has done in their lives.

VOTING INTO THE CHURCH. Particularly a Baptist custom. Voting by voice is followed by offering the penitent "the right hand of fellowship" and then baptism.

things which are written therein. (REVELATION 1:3)

Catalogue of Drawings

About the Authors

Artist ELEANOR CREEKMORE DICKINSON's first REVIVAL! opened at Knoxville's Dulin Museum in the heart of revival country. After much critical acclaim and public interest at The Corcoran Gallery of Art, Washington, D.C., in 1970, Ms. Dickinson's REVIVAL! went on the road for two years. She currently teaches at the California College of Arts and Crafts in Oakland. Her work is in the permanent collections of many museums and institutions, among them The Corcoran Gallery of Art, The Library of Congress, and The National Collection of Fine Arts. She has had ten one-artist museum shows. Ms. Dickinson's drawings may also be seen in THE COMPLETE FRUIT COOKBOOK. A Tennessee native, she was born in Knoxville and studied at the University of Tennessee with C. Kermit Ewing.

Writer BARBARA BENZIGER also was born and raised in Knoxville where she first knew Eleanor Dickinson. Ms. Benziger attended her friend's opening at the Corcoran, caught the enthusiasm for REVIVAL!, and joined the project in its book format. In her contribution to REVIVAL!, she went back home, observing revival meetings firsthand and meeting most of the people quoted in the book. A graduate of the University of Tennessee, Ms. Benziger spent ten years editing children's books for a New York publisher. She currently does freelance writing and makes her home in New York City.

74 75 10 9 8 7 6 5 4 3 2 1